a photo journey to NEW YORK CITY

Contributing writers
Helen Brower
J.P. MacBean

Helen Brower is a New York–based writer whose work frequently covers the Big Apple's cultural and entertainment attractions for numerous publications. She is a member of the New York Travel Writers Association and a past officer of the Northeast chapter of the Society of American Travel Writers.

J.P. MacBean lives in New York City and contributes travel, food and restaurant articles to many publications, including Travel & Leisure, The New York Daily News and Horizon. His books on New York include "New York: Heart of the City." He is the former press director of the New York Convention & Visitors Bureau.

Photo credits:

Front cover: **D. Hallinan/FPG International**
Esto Photographics/Dan Cornish: 36 (left); **FPG International:** 42 (bottom left); Braniff: 89 (left); Bruce Byers: 59 (right); T. Craig: 72 (bottom); E. Gebhardt: 80 (right); Peter Gridley: 45 (right); Dennis Hallinan: 7, 42 (top right & center), 44 (top), 45 (left); Shinichi Kanno: 65 (top); Richard Laird: 8 (bottom), 20 (top), 36 (right), 39 (right), 42 (bottom right), 59 (center), 78 (right); Bill Losh: 80 (left); Marmel Studios: 22 (top); Terry Qing: 50; Jeffrey Sylvester: 32 (bottom); William Wisser: 60 (left); **International Stock Photography:** 77 (right); George Ancona: 28 (left), 30 (bottom), 34 (left); Mark Bolster: 86 (top); Robert Brow: 26, 28 (right), 46 (top), 47, 48 (right), 61 (right), 79 (right), 82 (top), 83, 84 (left), 90, 92, 93, 94; Johan Elbers: 60 (right); Paulo Fridman: 87 (right), 95 (bottom); Garofalo: 61 (left); Miwako Ikeda: 11 (bottom); Lonny Kalfus: 72 (top), Peter Krinninger: 95 (top); Ken Levinson: 88 (right); Randy Masser: 33 (left); Radie Nedlin: 13 (bottom); Stan Ries: 65 (bottom), 70 (right); Lindsay Silverman: 53 (left); Bill Stanton: 32 (top), 69 (right), 82 (bottom); Stockman: 25 (right); Peter Tenzer Studio: 51 (right), 79 (center), Scott Thode: 86 (bottom), 87 (left); **Moving Image/Francene Keepy:** 37; **Photri:** 19 (bottom), 20 (bottom), 38 (right), 54 (left), 88 (left); Lani: 33 (right); Richard Nowitz: 51 (left); Stim: 4 (right center); William Kulik: 14; **Rainbow & Stars:** 76 (right); **The Rainbow Room:** 74; **Martha Swope Associates/Carol Rosegg:** 46 (bottom); **Michael Tamborrino:** 8 (top), 9, 10 (bottom), 21, 22 (bottom), 23, 24, 25 (left), 27, 29, 34 (right), 35 (right), 38 (left), 39 (left), 40, 41, 42 (top left), 48 (left), 49, 52, 53 (right), 54 (right), 55, 56, 57, 58 (left), 63 (left), 64, 67 (right), 69 (left), 75, 76 (left), 77 (left), 79 (left), 81, 84 (right), 85, 91, 92, 96; **Uniphoto:** 13 (top), 16, 19 (top), 31; Robert M. Anderson: 44 (bottom), 70 (left), 73; Orin Cassill: 6; Paul Conklin: 4 (bottom right); Dallas & John Heaton: 11 (top); Henryk T. Kaiser: 4 (top left & left center), 43, 89 (right); Ken Kaminsky: 78 (left); Don Katchusky: 4 (top right); Kit Kittle: 17 (right); George Kleiman: 15 (top), 18, 58 (right); Stuart Krasner: 30 (top); Jim Levitt: 10 (top); Pictor International: 4 (bottom left), 15 (bottom), 59 (left), 62, 63 (right), 66, 71; Lindsay Silverman: 12, 17 (left), 68; John Zoiner: 67 (left); **Paul Warchol:** 35 (left).

For AAA: Alex Gamble, Director, Consumer Publications; Jeanne Alonge, Senior Associate Editor.

Prepared for the American Automobile Association by Publications International, Ltd., 7373 North Cicero Avenue, Lincolnwood, IL 60646.

Copyright © 1991 by the American Automobile Association, 1000 AAA Drive, Heathrow, FL 32746-5063.
ISBN: 1-56251-012-6

CONTENTS

A MESSAGE FROM AAA

New York, New York. As the song says, it's the city that never sleeps. Stroll through Greenwich Village at four in the morning and you're likely to see more activity than you'd find in most cities at four in the afternoon.

Whatever else you think about New York, one thing is certain. The city has *character.*

From Brooklyn to Little Italy, New York boasts the sounds, smells and flavors of a dozen cultures. Try a kosher hot dog at a local deli, a thick slice of pizza at an Italian pizzeria or a spicy-hot Indian dish purchased from a sidewalk vendor.

Visit newly restored Ellis Island and relive the hopes and fears of the 12 million immigrants who entered America through those halls. Stand in the shadow of the Statue of Liberty and read the words of Emma Lazarus: "Give me your tired, your poor, your huddled masses yearning to breathe free."

Delight in a classical concert at Carnegie Hall, world-famous opera at the Metropolitan Opera House, high-kicking Rockettes routines at Radio City Music Hall or an award-winning triumph on Broadway.

Discover history at the Gracie Mansion or Grant's Tomb. Enjoy fast-paced buying and selling at the New York Stock Exchange. See the world through an artist's eyes at the Metropolitan Museum and the Museum of Modern Art.

There's more to see and do here than most can manage in a single visit. So the American Automobile Association is proud to offer this sampling of New York's finest.

Consumer Publications
American Automobile Association

Statue of Liberty

The Lady in the Harbor is America's most cherished symbol of freedom, but getting this gift from the people of France to the United States and up on her pedestal in New York Harbor wasn't always smooth sailing.

France's decision to present the United States with the statue was inspired by feelings of mutual affection generated by support for each other's revolutions. A Franco-American friendship group in France decided to celebrate that friendship with a gift symbolizing the two nations' common ideals, and sculptor Frédéric-Auguste Bartholdi was asked to come up with some ideas.

In 1871, on his first trip to the United States, Bartholdi sailed into New York Harbor, took one look, and knew he had found the perfect backdrop for the statue he had in mind: "Liberty Enlightening the World." Back in France he finished his other projects and in 1875 began the herculean task of building the immense statue that would stand at the gateway to America.

It took Bartholdi nine years to complete work and much touch-and-go fund-raising to support the project and pay for its transport from Europe to the United States, but finally on June 17, 1885, the statue sailed into the port of New York (Bartholdi followed a few months later in November). To help raise funds for the pedestal, Emma Lazarus wrote her famous poem "The New Colossus." A copy of the poem, whose most famous lines are "Give me your tired, your poor, your huddled masses yearning to breathe free," was placed in the statue's base in 1903.

On Dedication Day, October 28, 1886, thousands of people converged on Lower Manhattan for a look at Bedloe's Island (the original name of Liberty Island) and the Lady in the Harbor. President Grover Cleveland presided over ceremonies that included a parade of ships and displays of American and French flags. Also on hand were local politicians and a French delegation that included Bartholdi.

Finally, midway during a pause in a congressman's interminable speech, a cord attached to the veil covering the statue's face was pulled, revealing the "goddess" in all her glory. Jubilation broke forth, and the rest of the day was devoted to cannon salutes, waving of flags, ringing of bells and, of course, more speeches.

One hundred years later the festivities marking the Statue of Liberty's centennial were just as jubilant, if not more so. The celebrations got under way on July 4, 1986, and were led by President and Mrs. Reagan and the guests of honor, President and Mrs. François Mitterrand of France. The festivities featured a parade of tall ships, street fairs, fireworks, air and boat races, cultural events and the swearing in of new American citizens. On October 28

equally festive celebrations were held for the rededication ceremony.

The statue's 100th birthday celebrations followed an $85 million restoration that was carried out under the watchful eye of Lee Iacocca, Chrysler chairman and chairman of the Ellis Island–Statue of Liberty Foundation. Appropriately enough both French and American workmen contributed to the restoration work.

In her right hand the statue now carries a new copper torch with a gilded copper flame, based on Bartholdi's design. You can still see the original one; it's on display in the American Museum of Immigration at the base of the statue. New copper sheathing was added to spruce up the patina of the statue's skin. The crown was fitted with new stairs and 25 new windows, for safety reasons as well as to improve viewing. New elevators were installed, and access for handicapped visitors was improved.

Although Bartholdi deserves every bit of credit for the design and building of the statue, it was Gustave Eiffel—of Eiffel Tower fame—who devised the statue's support system, which was technologically advanced for its time. His engineering genius led him to create a system that allowed the statue to adjust to the expansions and contractions created by heat, cold and changes in wind directions. Though repairs and replacements were made during the restoration, Eiffel's design has held up remarkably well for more than 100 years.

Registry Room

Ellis Island National Monument

Reopened in the fall of 1990 after a $140 million restoration that started in 1984, Ellis Island celebrates its 100th anniversary in 1992. This stirring reminder of America's immigrant past stands in New York Harbor, just a few hundred yards from another celebrated monument, the Statue of Liberty.

What started out at the end of the 19th century as a few acres of uncultivated land grew into 27.5 acres consisting mostly of landfill and encompassing 33 buildings for the processing of new immigrants. During the years from 1892 to 1954 more than 17 million people made Ellis Island their port of entry into the United States. The men, women and children who arrived through this federal facility in those years represent the greatest human migration in modern times. Historians calculate that more than 40 percent—or at least 100 million—of all Americans alive today can trace their heritage to an immigrant ancestor who passed through Ellis Island's portals.

The American Immigrant Wall of Honor

As air travel became more common, however, Ellis Island fell into disuse as an immigration entry point. In 1965 Ellis Island was declared part of the Statue of Liberty National Monument, which is overseen by the National Park Service, a division of the U.S. Department of the Interior. In 1982 President Reagan asked Chrysler chief Lee Iacocca to establish and head up the Statue of Liberty–Ellis Island Foundation to raise funds for the restoration and preservation of both monuments.

The centerpiece of the restored monument is the Ellis Island Museum of Immigration, which offers a moving look at the immigrant experience through special exhibits, historic artifacts, old photographs and their own taped reminiscences. The museum, which is located in the 200,000-square-foot Main Building, features four major theme areas:

The Peopling of America. This display includes several freestanding exhibits that show Ellis Island in relation to the overall American immigration story. It is situated in the original, 9,300-square-foot Railroad Ticket Office and contains large maps, charts, graphs and displays that spotlight nearly 400 years of immigrant history.

The Ellis Island Processing Area. This 14-room exhibition wing depicts various facets of the immigration receiving process through such period memorabilia as old photographs, written diaries, oral histories and other items. The topics covered include Arrival, Board of Special Inquiry, Medical Inspection, Mental Testing, and—finally—Free to Land.

A touching exhibit here called Isle of Hope, Isle of Tears tells the sad stories of those would-be immigrants (representing less than 2 percent of the total) who were turned back because of poor health or other reasons.

The Peak Immigration Years—1892 to 1924. Highlighting the years when the bulk of the immigrants came to America, this exhibit portrays the step-by-step process from leaving the old country to integration into American society. Special exhibits here include Leaving the Homeland, Across the Land, The Closing Door and At Work in America.

The Ellis Island Galleries. These are divided into three sections. U.S. Government Property traces the history of Ellis Island; Treasures from Home is a fascinating collection of personal items that immigrants carried with them from their homelands; and Silent Voices tells the story of the restoration of Ellis Island.

Several study areas here allow visitors to enjoy hundreds of taped reminiscences and oral histories. A Library for Immigration Studies holds books, original manuscripts, photographs and microfiche.

In addition the museum houses two theaters with continuous showings of films about immigrants that feature old stills as well as contemporary footage.

Don't forget to look at the American Immigrant Wall of Honor, located just off the Great Hall next to the historic Registry Room. Modern-day Americans have donated funds to honor their ancestors by having their names placed on the wall.

Staten Island Ferry

It doesn't cost a nickel each way anymore, but at 50 cents round-trip, this is probably the most scenic cruise in the world for the money. Each ferry seats from 1,250 to 6,000 people and takes up to 45 automobiles. The ferries run every day, all year, and cross from Staten Island to Manhattan in about 20 minutes.

Amenities include both enclosed and open-air decks, rest rooms, a snack bar, separate smoking areas and, a holdover from the old days, itinerant shoeshine men on practically every trip.

Families and tourists predominate on Sundays, but on weekdays the ferries are packed to capacity at rush hours with Staten Islanders who are off to work or school or to shop in "the city."

Though Staten Islanders might look on their ferry as just another means of transportation, others have been moved to rapturous flights of romance and poetry. Hollywood movies are full of couples who fall in love watching the twinkling lights of nocturnal Manhattan approaching from the deck of the Staten Island Ferry. And we can only imagine what happened to Edna St. Vincent Millay on the Staten Island Ferry that prompted her to write the poem "Recuerdo," which begins: "We were very tired, we were very merry. We had gone back and forth all night on the ferry."

New York Vietnam Veterans Memorial

The memorial, dedicated on May 6, 1985, is located in Vietnam Veterans Plaza (formerly called Jeanette Park) in Lower Manhattan. Architects Peter Wormser and William Fellows created a translucent wall of greenish blocks, and writer John Ferrandino and others etched on it writings about the Vietnam veterans. Fragments of letters, diaries and poems by many soldiers who died in the war poignantly express their feelings.

The move to build a Vietnam Veterans Memorial in New York started in 1982 under then-Mayor Ed Koch, who established a Vietnam Veterans Memorial Commission. The commission was asked to arrange a competition for the memorial's design and also to create a job-training program for the veterans. In setting guidelines for the memorial, the commission made it clear that the purpose was not to express approval or disapproval of the war, but simply to make viewers aware of enduring human values. Approximately 1,200 veterans responded to the open competition, and out of their replies came a book, "Dear America," which is a collection of Vietnam War veterans' letters.

The memorial is best viewed at sunset, when the interior lights that illuminate the monument are fused with the natural fading light of the day.

New York Stock Exchange

Twenty-four brokers met in 1792 under a buttonwood tree in Lower Manhattan and agreed to form the New York Stock Exchange. The agreement was formalized on May 17, 1792, at the Tontine Coffee House. Congress had issued $80 million worth of stock in 1789 and 1790 to pay Revolutionary War debts. An official marketplace was needed in order to handle this stock.

The neo-Renaissance building that houses the New York Stock Exchange today is located at 8 Broad St., near Wall Street and about a block from historic Trinity Church. Completed in 1903, it replaced an 1865 building that stood on the same site. The new building's facade, which was constructed from a design by Trowbridge and Livingston, resembles an ancient Greek temple. Its Corinthian columns and pilasters are topped by a pediment with 11 figures depicting "Integrity Protecting the Works of Man." In 1922 a 22-story wing was added at the Wall Street side.

The enormous marble trading floor where the action takes place is about two-thirds the size of a football field. Buy and sell orders from the exchange's roughly 1,700 member firms are handled at 14 computer-equipped trading stations. From the glass-enclosed gallery overlooking the floor, you can listen to taped narrations and watch the sometimes frantic goings-on. The brokers are the ones in yellow jackets; the pages wear light blue jackets and the reporters wear navy blue jackets.

Don't forget to stop in at the New York Stock Exchange Visitors Center, whose entrance is at 20 Broad St. Here you can learn about the workings of the stock market by viewing exhibits, a film, a live presentation and by punching up questions on computer terminals.

World Trade Center

The World Trade Center is usually referred to as the twin towers because its two 110-story primary towers rise 1,350 feet, making them the tallest buildings in New York City. But the complex also includes a 47-story office building, two nine-story office buildings, the eight-story U.S. Customhouse and the 22-story Vista International Hotel. The complex is situated on a 16-acre site in Lower Manhattan and is connected to its neighbor, the World Financial Center, by an overhead bridge.

All the World Trade Center structures are built around a central five-acre landscaped plaza, and they're all interconnected by a lower-level pedestrian area, where most of the shops and the Market Square restaurants are located.

The complex is owned and operated by the Port Authority of New York and New Jersey and has been open for business since December 1970. This awesome city-within-a-city is home to more than 1,200 government agencies and companies of all descriptions. About 60,000 people work here every day. Many of them arrive by one of the subway lines that feed right into the buildings, then zoom up to their offices in one of the World Trade Center's 99 elevators. Close to 100,000 additional people visit here for business, shopping, dining and sightseeing.

The World Trade Center's most famous tenant, Windows on the World, offers dining, dancing and dazzling views from the 107th floor of No. 1 World Trade Center. On the 106th floor are Windows' smaller dining rooms and a ballroom used for private functions. About a dozen television stations in the metropolitan area rely on the 360-foot television mast at the top of No. 1 World Trade Center to transmit their programs in all kinds of weather.

Every year about 1.5 million people take the elevator up to the observation deck on the 107th floor of No. 2 World Trade Center to enjoy unforgettable cityscapes. A rooftop promenade, at 1,377 feet, is the highest outdoor viewing platform in the world. You'll also find a History of Trade Exhibit, a restaurant and a gift shop.

Artworks by such famous painters and sculptors as Alexander Calder, Louise Nevelson and Joan Miro are displayed on the Tower Mezzanine levels and on the outdoor Plaza, which is also the setting for lunchtime jazz and pop concerts in summer.

floor that is graced by 16 towering, live Washingtonia robusta palm trees.

The Winter Garden is the main venue for the center's marvelous Arts & Events program. There's almost always something going on—lunchtime concerts, evening and holiday dance performances and weekend art shows and theatrical events.

In spring and summer arts programs are also offered on the Plaza, a park bordering the North Cove Yacht Harbor, and the Courtyard, a three-story, glass-roofed facility surrounded by balconies. Also in the Battery Park City complex, of which the World Financial Center is the core, is the Esplanade, a 1.2-mile-long waterfront park with street lights and benches to attract strollers; the 7-acre North Park, which has a children's playground; and two urban oases, Rector Park and the South Gardens. The soon-to-open Museum of Jewish Heritage will be a memorial to the Holocaust.

World Financial Center

The four sleek office towers that make up the World Financial Center are the hub of the new, multi-use Battery Park City in Lower Manhattan. The retail-office complex was designed by the architectural firm of Cesar Pelli & Associates and developed by Canada's Olympia & York. A fifth tower is slated to open soon, which will give the complex a total of 8 million square feet of office space and 350,000 square feet of retail shops, restaurants and other establishments.

What makes the World Financial Center unique is the innovative way the designers have interwoven its commercial facilities with public spaces, making it not just a great place for corporate headquarters, but also one of New York's most exciting new people places.

The jewel in the crown of the center is the public entertainment venue, the Winter Garden. This dazzling, 120-foot-high vaulted glass and steel edifice is just about the same size as Grand Central Terminal's main waiting room. It has a spectacular grand staircase and a marble

Empire State Building

It's no longer the tallest building in the world, but it's still the most famous and the one that immediately comes to mind when we hear the word "skyscraper." A symbol of the boundless optimism of America, the Empire State Building opened on May 1, 1931, during the height of the Great Depression.

In order to make room for the awesome, 102-story building, another famous landmark, the Waldorf-Astoria Hotel, was forced to move from its original location at Fifth Avenue and 34th Street to its present address on Park Avenue between 49th and 50th streets.

It's impossible to talk about the Empire State Building without mentioning statistics. The limestone and steel tower is 1,250 feet from its toes right up to the 102nd floor. (If you count the lightning rod on top, it's 1,454 feet.) The building weighs a staggering 365,000 tons, is equipped with 3,500 miles of telephone and telegraph wire, and has 6,500 windows and 73 elevators. Every February, members of the Road Runners Club race up 1,575 steps to the building's 86th floor.

An outdoor promenade and indoor observation deck is on the 86th floor, and a closed observatory is on the 102nd floor. On a clear day you can enjoy a dazzling, 360-degree view that can stretch 80 miles—all the way north to the Bronx, west to the New Jersey Palisades, south to Staten Island and east to the United Nations and the East River.

In the summer of 1945, before the practice of lighting the tower started, a World War II plane, flying in dense fog, crashed into the building. Although the top of the skyscraper was encased in flames and 14 people were killed, the tragedy could have been much worse if the accident hadn't occurred on a Sunday, when offices were closed.

The Empire State Building has been the star of many movies, but it's probably best remembered for the scene in the original, 1933 version of "King Kong" when the lovesick gorilla is shot down from his perch on the building's mast by circling airplanes. The unfortunate gorilla can be seen in one of several free exhibits in the building. You can also see an Eight Wonders of the World exhibit and the Guinness World Record Exhibit Hall on the main level, where weird and wonderful achievements are celebrated.

New York Public Library

If any building has come to symbolize old New York's graceful public buildings, it's the New York Public Library's main branch at Fifth Avenue and 42nd Street. It's one of five New York Public Library branches that have been declared historic landmark buildings. This one has a particularly interesting history.

The building started out not as a public institution but as the merger of three private libraries. It was built from 1898 to 1911 on the site of the Croton Reservoir to house the extensive Astor, Lenox and Tilden collections. Its designers were the prestigious architectural firm of Carrère & Hastings, which was much in demand among New York's elite around the turn of the century.

The library has more than 200 rooms in all, and it has about 29 million books, manuscripts, photographs, paintings and other materials, making it one of America's great research institutions. It's the third largest library in the United States, after the Library of Congress in Washington and the Widener Library at Harvard.

It also has some of New York's most monumental interior spaces. Be sure to walk through the Gottesman Hall on the main floor, where about 10 major exhibitions are held every year; the vast Main Reading Room on the third floor; the Salomon Room, with fine art objects from the library's own collections; and the Bartos Forum.

Eternal budget crunches have contributed to making the library a delightful mix of high-tech and stick-in-the-mud old-fashioned. A recently installed computerized system calls up titles from the library's enormous research collection, but the pneumatic tube device that was installed in 1911 remains in use elsewhere, and it works fine.

Flanking the main entrance of this French Beaux Arts–style building are two of the coolest cats in town—the imperturbable stone lions nicknamed Patience and Fortitude. Every Christmas these two much-photographed charmers are decked out in big red bows and Yuletide wreaths. On balmy days in summer you're likely to see the lunchtime crowd brown-bagging it on the steps leading up to the entrance, while sidewalk entertainers audition for the big time by testing their magic tricks, juggling talents and Michael Jackson imitations on their peers.

United Nations

Ever since it started rising on an 18-acre tract of land on the East River, the United Nations has been the center of heated controversy. The topic might concern politics, architecture or the diplomatic status of its high-ranking officials—who at times seem to be immune to the laws that ordinary mortals are expected to obey. Still there's no denying that the United Nations has become one of the most compelling must-see visitor attractions in the Big Apple.

During those heady post–World War II days when the concept of "One World" had captured imaginations of many people, John D. Rockefeller, Jr., purchased this six-block

plot of land running from 42nd to 48th streets for $8.5 million and donated the land to the United Nations. The construction of the U.N. buildings started in the early 1950s under the guidance of a team of internationally renowned architects that included Oscar Niemeyer, who designed Brasilia; Sven Markelius of Sweden; an American, Wallace K. Harrison; and the famous French architect Le Corbusier. Although the overall design concept is generally credited to Le Corbusier, he quit the project before it was completed and left it to Harrison's firm of Harrison & Abramovitz to take up where he had left off.

The United Nations's main structures are the 39-story glass-and-marble Secretariat, where the staffs of member nations have their offices; the white limestone General Assembly Building, where members meet when the United Nations is in session; and the low-rise Conference Building, which houses the media, conference rooms and support services.

A conducted tour of the United Nations is very highly recommended, especially if you want to navigate your way smoothly. The tours are offered daily in several languages and operate frequently. A limited number of free tickets are available to the General Assembly's open sessions.

Visitors usually enter through the General Assembly Building, under the flags of member nations. You'll probably pass through one of the seven nickel-bronze doors donated by Canada. Inside are breathtaking stained-glass windows by Chagall; murals by Leger and Tamayo; the Foucault Pendulum, which shows the rotation of the Earth and was a gift from the Netherlands; the Soviet Union's *Sputnik,* launched in 1957; and a moon rock that was retrieved by the Apollo 14 astronauts during their 1971 lunar expedition.

The United Nations houses more art treasures and arts and crafts of the peoples of the world than many museums.

You'll see paintings and sculptures by Georges Rouault, Henry Moore, Barbara Hepworth, Salvador Dali and Candido Portinari, as well as a handwoven Persian carpet donated by the late Shah of Iran, a Japanese peace bell, a Belgian tapestry, a beautiful ivory carving from China, a silk wall covering from Ghana and other gifts.

In addition, the tranquil, beautifully landscaped United Nations garden, just inside the entrance gates to the complex, holds statues inspired by heroic themes that were created by sculptors from many nations.

The U.N. Gift Center on the lower level of the General Assembly building offers a wide assortment of items from around the globe, including jewelry, decorative items, dolls, laceware and embroidery, lacquerware, ceramics and traditional arts and crafts. Also worth a visit is the United Nations bookstore, where you can purchase books about the United Nations and its operations, children's books, posters, postcards and the popular UNESCO Christmas cards that benefit children of the world. If there are stamp collectors in the family, you'll want to pick up some of the commemorative issues that can be purchased at the United Nations Post Office, located right on the premises.

Despite all the security and safety precautions, you might be pleasantly surprised to learn that the Delegates' Dining Room in the Conference Building is open to the public for lunch. Ask for a pass from the Information Desk. Once inside the dining room, try to get a seat near the windows for a wonderful view overlooking the East River.

Above: Security Council
Right: General Assembly

Intrepid Sea-Air-Space Museum

When New York real-estate magnate Zachary Fisher heard that the former World War II aircraft carrier USS *Intrepid* was headed for the scrap heap, he quickly moved in and salvaged this bit of military history. Fisher led a group of like-minded citizens in overseeing the transformation of the ship into a living history museum of 20th-century military technology and lore.

The *Intrepid* started its new life as a museum in 1982, moored in the Hudson River at 46th Street. Its displays feature three naval vessels, 40 aircraft, more than 30 missiles and a collection of airplane and ship models. It's also the national headquarters for the Congressional Medal of Honor Society.

The section on naval vessels features an exhibit on the *Intrepid*'s military history, including its role in the Battle for Leyte Gulf, the largest naval battle in history. Also in this section are three halls that trace the role of military technology from the Spanish-American War up to the present.

One of the most popular exhibits is the guided missile submarine, the USS *Growler*. Its entire operating deck is open to the public, including the section that served as Top Secret Missile Command Center. The *Growler* is the only nuclear-missile-firing submarine on display in the world.

The destroyer USS *Edson* is reputed to be the best example of a restored military vessel in America. Named for Gen. "Red Mike" Edson, a World War II marine hero and Medal of Honor winner, the *Edson* saw combat in Vietnam.

Forty aircraft are on display, most of them located on the *Intrepid*'s hangar and flight decks. The most impressive is the U.S. Air Force's spectacular Lockheed A-12 Blackbird high-speed reconnaissance plane, the largest aircraft in the museum and the world's fastest.

The museum has an extensive collection of missiles. Among the more recent additions are a "Scudbuster" Patriot and the wreckage of a Scud missile from the Persian Gulf War. The collection also includes Tomahawk, Harpoon, Sidewinder, Sparrow and Phoenix missiles.

South Street Seaport

The South Street Seaport Museum is a restoration of an area of Lower Manhattan that was the center of New York City's thriving maritime industry in the 19th century. The seaport has hundreds of restored shops, houses and eateries, but the real focal point of the complex is the wonderful old sailing ships. You can climb aboard and explore some of them. The historic vessels include the lightship *Ambrose,* whose job was to guide other ships safely to port, a small wooden tugboat, a restored 1885 three-masted tall ship, a 1925 steam commuter ferry and a Gloucester fishing schooner.

Regular or chartered sails of New York harbor are offered on some of the seaport's ships, including the four-masted, 347-foot *Peking;* the 19th-century paddle wheeler *Andrew Fletcher;* the steamboat *DeWitt Clinton;* and the two-masted schooner *Pioneer.*

The centerpiece of the seaport's historic buildings is Schermerhorn Row. This series of interconnected 19th-century buildings with sloping roofs and high chimneys now houses restaurants and boutiques. Pier 17 and the Fulton Market Building are each three-story structures that feature an assortment of seafood restaurants, food stalls selling fresh fish and produce, and specialty shops and boutiques.

Cannon's Walk is a block of 19th- and 20th-century buildings with a theater and courtyard. Just adjacent is a group of establishments collectively known as "The Shops on Front Street," where some of the seaport's trendiest boutiques and galleries are located.

If you're an early riser, you should take an early morning tour of the famous Fulton Fish Market and watch the catch of the day being prepared. Follow that up with a visit to "The Seaport Experience" at the Trans-Lux Seaport Theater to see a multi-screen show on the history of New York. Then watch craftsmen fashion ship models at the Maritime Crafts Center, learn how a 19th-century print shop operated at Bowne & Co. Stationers, and shop for old navigational charts at the Edmund M. Blunt Book & Chart Store.

At lunchtime on weekdays many of the restaurants are filled with workers from nearby Wall Street offices. The area is also popular on weekends, especially in summer, when outdoor jazz concerts are given on the pier and jugglers, fire-eaters and others entertain on the plaza.

Radio City Music Hall

One of New York's great Art Deco treasures, Radio City Music Hall is the home of the Rockettes and the Mighty Wurlitzer. The Music Hall, which is part of the Rockefeller Center complex, opened in 1932. With close to 6,000 seats in its main auditorium, Radio City Music Hall was the biggest theater in the world. Nowadays Radio City is frequently used for concerts starring pop and rock musical artists. However, it started out as a variety show hall. Later, in its heyday, New Yorkers and visitors came to the Music Hall to see first-run movies on its giant screen, followed by exciting stage shows.

If there were an award for "America's Most Beloved Showplace," the Music Hall would win hands down. It's got everything—a stage that goes up and down, three big movie screens and a gold contour curtain that weighs three tons. Its symphony orchestra is led by a conductor who is so imbued with the spirit of show business that he often waves his lighted baton facing the audience, rather than the musicians.

The magnificent interior of Radio City Music Hall is a symphony of mirrored walls, striking art works, huge murals, plush carpets, a 50-foot-high foyer and three mezzanine levels artfully arranged to offer theatergoers the most breathtaking views.

At one time Radio City boasted a painting by the American artist Stuart Davis. It graced the walls of the men's room on the lower level, which would be sacrilege anywhere but at the Music Hall, where the rest rooms are more lavish than many palaces. The painting was moved some years ago to the Museum of Modern Art.

The behind-the-scenes action at Radio City is almost as fascinating as the action on the 144-by-66-foot stage. The conducted one-hour behind-the-scenes tour includes a visit to and explanation of the backstage areas, the recording studio, the rehearsal hall, the costume rooms, and the technical and special effects equipment. You'll see expert technicians who are constantly on the alert to be sure that special sound-and-light effects and split-second timing required for some of the Music Hall's complex productions all work perfectly.

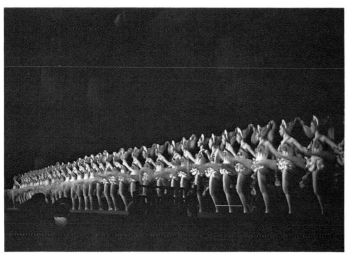

Brooklyn Botanic Garden

The 52-acre Brooklyn Botanic Garden was founded on city land in 1910 and has since grown to become one of the most outstanding urban gardens in America.

Just adjacent to the Brooklyn Museum and about a 15-minute subway ride from midtown Manhattan, the Brooklyn Botanic Garden holds plants, flowers and trees of every description. Represented are plant species indigenous to the United States as well as exotic blooms from distant lands.

The Cranford Rose Garden, which opened in 1927, boasts more than 5,000 rose bushes, representing 800 varieties. The Shakespeare Garden has some 80 varieties of plants, all of which are mentioned in the great bard's plays. The Local Floral Section, which represents eight ecological zones, contains only plants that grow within 100 miles of New York City.

The Japanese gardens include the Bonsai Garden, Cherry Blossom Garden, and Japanese Hill and Pond Garden, which was designed in 1914 by a famous Japanese garden landscaper. The garden has a traditional Japanese teahouse overlooking a stream filled with goldfish. It also contains an ancient lantern that was a gift from the people of Tokyo to the people of New York as a symbol of their sister-city relationship.

You can also see an herb garden, a fragrance garden for the blind, a hands-on rock garden and a children's garden, where young people can learn how to grow vegetables.

Special holiday and seasonal events are staged in the various gardens, most often to celebrate the annual arrival of a particular flower or plant. The Cherry Blossom Festival, for example, is celebrated in early May, roses take center stage from June to October, and the arrival of autumn is marked every year with a brilliant display of fall foliage.

Inside, the Conservatory has botanical exhibits on flowers, plants and trees of the world. There are also lecture series and special programs for adults and children.

MAJOR ATTRACTIONS FOR CHILDREN

Bronx Zoo

Since the Bronx Zoo, America's largest urban zoo, was founded in 1899, it has served as one of the world's great wildlife sanctuaries and as a haven for vanishing species. In order to see some of the animals who live at the Bronx Zoo in their original habitats, you'd have to travel 30,000 miles. More than 4,000 animals are in the collection, representing nearly 700 different species. Every year close to 1,000 baby animals are born at the zoo.

The Bronx Zoo has 265 acres of green parklands where many animals roam free. Special exhibit sections re-create the plant and wildlife environments of many regions of the world.

Wild Asia is one of the most popular sections at the zoo and one that has inspired a host of imitators since it opened in 1977. It consists of Jungle World and Wild Asia Plaza, where about 250 bird species and 16 animal species are in residence.

Between May and October climb aboard the Bengali Express, a monorail that takes you on a two-mile, 25-minute narrated safari through the forests of Wild Asia. Except for an occasional peek through the trees at a Bronx apartment building, the wonderful attention to detail in re-creating an Asian jungle will convince you that you've been magically transported to an exotic environment thousands of miles away. During the ride you'll have an opportunity to see Asian elephants, Siberian tigers, the shy red panda (usually spied hiding behind the shrubbery), rhino, rare sika deer and antelopes. In summer Wild Asia also has camel rides and animal demonstrations in the Wildlife Theater.

Jungle World features an indoor rain forest and a variety of animals from the tropical jungles of South Asia. Enjoying the lush foliage and the humidity here are proboscis monkeys swinging from the trees, snoozing crocodiles and almost 800 other animals, most of whom roam free and are separated from viewers only by rocky cliffs, tropical waterfalls and streams.

Although all of the Bronx Zoo is a paradise for kids, its Children's Zoo is a standout—one of the best in the United States. Youngsters can learn all about animals by getting to know them. They can discover what it feels like to be a hatching baby bird by sitting in a bird nest. They can test their jumping skills against those of a bullfrog, slip into a turtle shell, slither down a tree like a lizard, and crawl through a prairie dog tunnel. The kids can also pet and feed the domestic animals.

The World of Darkness presents a fascinating look at nocturnal animals. Day is turned into night in about 25 displays with such names as Wings Into the Night and The Forest After Dark. In the dimly lit hall you'll be able to make out such well-known creatures of the night as bats and owls, as well as porcupines, skunks and leopard cats.

Other exhibits well worth seeing are the Himalayan Highlands, home of the beautiful, endangered snow leopard; the Elephant House, which recently reopened after a renovation; Bird Valley and the World of Birds, with hundreds of bird species, including some that have disappeared from the wild; and one of the newest sections, the MouseHouse, where you can learn about the nicer side of this much maligned rodent.

If the kids get cranky from walking between exhibits, you can take the Skyfari aerial tramway or the Safari train, which travels between Wild Asia and the Children's Zoo.

The Bronx Zoo is operated by the New York Zoological Society and offers wonderful educational programs for children. It's open all year, although some of the individual exhibits are closed during certain seasons or for renovations.

Hayden Planetarium and Naturemax Theater

The Hayden Planetarium, on the north side of the American Museum of Natural History building, has been delighting children since 1935. The copper dome on the outside is a promise of outer-space thrills to come on the inside.

The most popular attractions in the planetarium—and the ones that elicit the most oohs and aahs from the youngsters—are the three-dimensional sky shows that take place in the Sky Theater on the second floor. The dome is 75 feet in diameter and 48 feet from the floor. More than 100 computer-controlled special-effects projectors take you on a celestial voyage of discovery.

The first-floor Guggenheim Space Theater shows wraparound slide presentations on a series of 22 screens. Exhibits compare the relative sizes of the various planets and satellites. On display in the adjacent galleries are meteorites. The most astounding of these is the Ahnighito meteorite, discovered in the wastelands of Greenland, which weighs in at a hefty 68,000 pounds.

The planetarium also has permanent and changing exhibits on the development of astronomy and on astronomical facts and fantasies. Special exhibits include the Hall of Sun, the Laserium, the Blacklight Gallery and Astronomia. Also on display is the 14-ton Willamette meteorite.

The planetarium's Sky Theater schedules special shows throughout the year and such annual favorites as the "Christmas Star Show." There are also lectures and educational programs. Special shows for preschoolers feature toddlers' favorites, such as the Sesame Street Muppets, and, for teens, Friday and Saturday laser shows are accompanied by rock music.

There are also a number of hands-on exhibits, a good reference library and a shop that specializes in space-age gifts.

The Naturemax Theater, also in the American Museum of Natural History, boasts what it claims is New York City's biggest movie screen. It's four stories high and more than 60 feet wide and is augmented by a six-channel sound system. The films shown here explore the workings of nature, the human body and the universe. On Friday and Saturday evenings, the theater schedules double features.

New York Philharmonic Young People's Concerts

The New York Philharmonic's special programs for young people are a great way for parents to expand their kids' musical horizons from MTV to the world of the great classics. Although some of the programs—such as the lecture and demonstration series offered in local schools—have been created specifically for New York–area schoolchildren, others can also be enjoyed by visiting youngsters.

Primary among these are the Young People's Concerts, a series of four programs offered every year at Lincoln Center's Avery Fisher Hall. The Young People's Concerts concept was originated by Leonard Bernstein. In their current form the presentations are geared to students of junior high school age. Themed performances created specifically for kids in this age group include "Young Performers," "The Symphony" and "Poetry in Music." In addition special programs enable high school students to attend a three-hour dress rehearsal of the New York Philharmonic and get caught up in the excitement shared by the musicians just hours before they're scheduled to play an evening performance.

Rockefeller Center Ice Skating Rink

Since it opened on Christmas Day in 1936, the ice skating rink on Rockefeller Center's Lower Plaza has been graced by the world's most famous ice skaters—Sonja Henie, Dick Button, Robin Cousins, Tai Babalonia and Randy Gardner, Peggy Fleming, Torville and Dean, and Brian Boitano.

One of the Big Apple's most photographed sights, the 122-foot-long, 59-foot-wide rink attracts about 100,000 skaters of all levels of expertise every year. It's open from October through April (the rest of the year, it's transformed into an outdoor restaurant) and has more than five miles of pipe permanently installed beneath its terrazzo floor to maintain a smooth ice surface. About once a month free lunchtime ice shows featuring top amateur and professional skaters take place on the ice skating rink.

The rink is lovely at dusk as skaters swirl around the ice under the famous gold-leaf statue of Prometheus, but it's even more beautiful during the Yuletide holidays, when it's graced by the famous Rockefeller Center Christmas tree.

Central Park Zoo

The Central Park Zoo underwent a renovation and reconstruction from 1985 to 1988 that transformed it from a ho-hum facility to one of the Big Apple's most exciting attractions for kids and their parents. Since 1864 the city of New York has always operated a small zoo of one kind or another at Fifth Avenue and 64th Street in Central Park. The original zoo consisted mainly of donated animals. With some improvements it later became the Central Park Menagerie. In 1934, under New York's visionary Parks Commissioner Robert Moses, the zoo was newly fitted out with red-brick animal houses and became the Central Park Zoo.

In 1980 the New York Zoological Society and the Georgia-based Wildlife Survival Center decided to work together to create a new state-of-the-art zoo on the site of the old one. Just about all of the existing buildings were demolished and replaced with completely new facilities.

In addition to being physically more attractive, the new Central Park Zoo meets rigorous standards set by wildlife professionals. For example, only species that can be cared for in the limited space available (about 5.5 acres) reside here. Even with that restriction, however, the zoo has about 450 animals representing 100 species. The zoo features diverse ecological habitats arranged according to climate zones: The Tropic Zone, Temperate Territory and Polar Circle are arranged around a garden.

The Tropic Zone is a skylighted octagonal building that re-creates the lush, fragile beauty of the tropical forests, particularly those of Central and South America. Birds, monkeys, reptiles and bats live in this jungle setting, complete with roaring waterfalls and trees.

The Temperate Territory has outdoor habitats for Asian and North American animals that are originally from climates like our own. They include Japanese macaques (snow monkeys), red pandas, waterfowl and river otters.

Perhaps the most enjoyable of all the zones is the Polar Circle, particularly the temperature-controlled Ice Pack building, inhabited by the amusing-looking chinstrap and gentoo penguins and their friends, the tufted puffins. Outside is a multilevel habitat where polar bears occasionally leave their perch on a rock for a swim.

Before leaving stop at the Wildlife Conservation Center and the Heckscher Zoo School, which has two classrooms and an auditorium—part of the zoo's ongoing efforts to educate youngsters about wildlife.

Coney Island

Coney Island is one of three neighborhoods, along with Brighton Beach and Manhattan Beach, that form a peninsula on the southern tip of Brooklyn. This legendary playground has been a haven for New Yorkers escaping the summer heat and crowds since the 1840s. It reached its heyday, however, when the railway began extending all the way to its sandy beaches in the 1870s. Development came quickly thereafter, with the opening of lavish Victorian-style resort hotels, the creation of the Brighton Race Track, and the introduction of a strange but tasty new culinary treat called the hot dog.

By the turn of the century, thousands of people were thronging to Coney Island for thrill-packed rides like the Steeplechase, spectacular sideshows, and exciting amusement parks like Dreamland and Luna Park. Coney Island–Brighton Beach became the place for New York–area families to go in the summer. They went to enjoy the surf, the healthful sea air, the bathhouses, long walks on the boardwalk, the summer stock theater presentations, elegant shops, superb restaurants and nightlife, and to catch glimpses of champion swimmers practicing their backstrokes.

In the years following World War II, however, New Yorkers found other places to spend their summers, and gradually Coney Island and its neighbors fell into a state of neglect. Many of the rides that had thrilled generations of schoolchildren closed, and the area became a veritable ghost town—except for two hardy survivors, which still stand: the original Nathan's Hot Dogs and the New York Aquarium (a tip—kids are crazy about the shark tank).

About two decades ago, however, in one of those demographic phenomena that no one can explain, Russian immigrants began arriving and settling here—so many, in fact, that the area's new nickname is "Little Odessa." The immigrants have put their own colorful stamp on the neighborhood by opening restaurants, shops and cabarets on and around Coney Island Avenue and thus reviving what was a dying part of the city. Nowadays if you stroll on the boardwalk on a balmy summer evening, you're likely to hear couples chatting in Russian while their children prattle in English and munch on hot dogs.

Wollman Memorial Rink

The Wollman Memorial Rink, located near Central Park, is 33,000 feet square and has a concrete base, below which lies its ice-making machinery. At one time the rink was used strictly for ice skating and was open only in winter, but a few seasons ago roller skating was introduced from spring through fall. About the only time the rink is closed, in fact, is when workmen are changing over from summer to winter by making ice and from winter to summer by preparing the ground for roller skating. Facilities for renting roller skates and ice skates and a snack bar are on the premises. The rink can also be rented for private events.

Another recent addition is an 18-hole miniature golf course called Gotham Golf. Every hole is marked with a plaque bearing the name of a famous New York building, bridge or other landmark. There's a La Guardia Airport, Lincoln Center, Bronx Zoo, Triborough Bridge and so on.

This beloved New York landmark had fallen into a state of neglect and badly needed a major refurbishment. When the project became mired in lengthy delays and high expenditures that far exceeded the original budget, tycoon Donald Trump stepped in and offered to complete the work. Trump got so attached to the rink during the project that his company, Trump Ice, now operates it in cooperation with the Ice Capades.

Brooklyn Children's Museum

The Brooklyn Children's Museum claims the title of the first children's museum. Founded in 1899, its goal has been to provide a setting where children and their parents can learn through first-hand experience. The museum has more than 20,000 artifacts and natural science specimens. Most of the exhibits have at least some hands-on components.

Continuing events are offered in three age categories. The 7-and-older crowd can enjoy about a half dozen activities, including a study of how stargazing has influenced the world's religions, origami-making (the Japanese art of folding paper into designs) and a chance to learn about inventions that were inspired by dreams.

The 4-and-older set can take a crash course in spelling their names using sign language, look at the reasons why some animals are nocturnal, and explore the laws of physics through block-building. Kids 2 and older learn how to handcraft simple items, explore bedtime rituals of the world through lullabies and bedtime stories, and play with amusing toys.

Technological displays introduce kids to the workings of a windmill, a steam engine and a greenhouse, and educational exhibits focus on minerals, shells, dolls, costumes and archaeological artifacts.

Jamaica Bay Wildlife Refuge

It's hard to imagine that a place like the Jamaica Bay Wildlife Refuge exists within a stone's throw of the office towers of Manhattan. Located on Cross Bay Boulevard between Howard Beach and Broad Channel in Queens, this is a place where people come to get away from it all.

The refuge consists of enormous man-made tidal wetlands and uplands that encompass more than 9,000 acres of land and water; in total, it's nearly as big as the entire island of Manhattan. It's one of the most important urban wildlife refuge places in the country. The areas that are open to the public are at the western end of the refuge.

There are two trails where you can enjoy birdwatching and nature walks all year round, seven days a week (except Christmas Day and New Year's Day), from dawn until dusk. More than 300 species of birds and small mammals make their home here, including waterfowl, predatory birds and songbirds. Almost as many species of plants are found here. On the weekends there are slide and film shows, followed by tours conducted by National Park Service Rangers. A good time to come is during the fall migratory season, which starts around the middle of August.

Metropolitan Museum of Art

More than 4 million people visit the Metropolitan Museum of Art annually, making it—according to some counts—the Big Apple's number one attraction. Founded by a group of wealthy New York art patrons and opened in 1870, the Met's vital statistics are enough to awe even the most jaded museum-goer. A team of about 2,200 full-time employees and 600 volunteers are needed to staff its 19 curatorial departments. Its collections total more than 2 million works of art, representing 5,000 years of cultural history.

The Temple of Dendur

You'd need at least a week to see all of the noteworthy works in the museum, but be sure not to miss the Temple of Dendur in the Egyptian Wing; El Greco's "View of Toledo" in the European Paintings section; the American Wing, with 25 period rooms and Tiffany glass windows; the Robert Lehman wing, with superb Italian paintings from the 14th and 15th centuries; the Lila Acheson Wallace gallery, featuring 8,000 modern works; the Michael C. Rockefeller Wing of Primitive Art; the Chinese and Japanese collections; and the Costume Institute, whose delightful changing exhibits pay tribute to the world of fashion.

Solomon R. Guggenheim Museum

The museum, with its swirling ramps that lead the viewer from one level to the next, is housed in the only public building designed by Frank Lloyd Wright in New York City. The eclectic collection drawn from the estate of the millionaire founder from which the museum takes its name formed the nucleus of the museum's works. These include what is generally regarded as the world's largest collection of Kandinsky paintings, as well as works by Picasso, Chagall, de Kooning and other European and American artists associated with the modern movement. The Justin K. Thannhauser wing consists of approximately 75 superb Impressionist and Postimpressionist paintings by Renoir, Cezanne, Gauguin, Van Gogh and others.

The museum recently added a new wing. Plans for the addition caused almost as much hoopla as the original building, which was variously described by critics as a snail, a bun and a large toilet bowl. In time the new gallery will undoubtedly become as beloved a fixture of Upper Fifth Avenue as the original building, which New Yorkers now affectionately refer to as "the Guggie."

Museum of Modern Art (MOMA)

MOMA is the pioneer art institution that led the way for other modern art museums. Its exhibits feature more than 100,000 works of art from a variety of media—painting, sculpture, architecture and design. The original MOMA building at 11 W. 53rd St. was expanded several years ago, nearly doubling the amount of its available exhibition space. The museum's famous holdings include Van Gogh's "The Starry Night"; Picasso's "Les Demoiselles d'Avignon"; Andrew Wyeth's "Christina's World" and Andy Warhol's "Gold Marilyn Monroe."

MOMA was the first major museum to recognize the role of film as a contemporary art form. Screenings of classic films, silent movies and other golden oldies from its collection of nearly 10,000 movies regularly lure movie buffs and film students. In summer the Abby Aldrich Rockefeller Sculpture Garden, which contains works by Rodin, Henry Moore, Picasso and others, is the site of free concerts. Smart New Yorkers who do their Christmas shopping at the city's excellent museum shops are especially fond of MOMA's shop, which features attractive objects in modern design in addition to reproductions, books and posters.

The Cloisters

The uptown branch of the Metropolitan Museum of Art houses a priceless collection of medieval art and architecture. Situated on a bluff overlooking the Hudson River, the Cloisters is easily accessible by public bus. It was built on land donated by John D. Rockefeller to accommodate the medieval columns and capitals amassed by the American sculptor George Grey Barnard while he was living in France. The stone building, surrounded by gardens, incorporates sections of five cloisters from medieval monasteries, a Romanesque chapel and a 12th-century Spanish apse. The museum's treasures include the Unicorn Tapestries and many illuminated manuscripts and medieval artifacts. Its barrel-vaulted rooms also contain the sarcophagi of medieval kings, statues of the Virgin and Christ and magnificent stained-glass windows. A visit to the Cloisters is especially affecting on a rainy day when the mist rises up from the Hudson and the building's stone walls and high-ceilinged rooms take on a deliciously brooding quality.

Whitney Museum of American Art

Although the Whitney is technically several museums with branches around the city and one in Connecticut, when people refer to the Whitney Museum, they usually mean the main branch at Madison Avenue and 75th Street. The original Whitney Museum was founded in 1930 by Gertrude Vanderbilt Whitney, a socialite sculptor and art patron. Her purpose was to help draw attention to struggling American artists and drum up sales of their works at a time when most wealthy Americans were collecting only European art.

The Whitney Museum's collection is strong on 20th-century art and features an extensive selection of contemporary sculpture as well as paintings. The collection includes famous works by Edward Hopper, Jackson Pollock, Thomas Hart Benton, Georgia O'Keeffe, Duane Hanson, Frank Stella, Andy Warhol, Willem de Kooning, Isamu Noguchi, Louise Nevelson, Red Grooms and many others. The Whitney Biennial Exhibition held every two years spotlights important new developments in the world of contemporary art and draws top art collectors and dealers from around the world.

American Museum of Natural History

Dioramas of mastodons lurking in primeval forests and lifelike replicas of dinosaurs have made this museum a great favorite of school groups for generations. The museum's 34 million artifacts trace human and animal evolution, the migrations of peoples of the world and the products of human creativity. Special wings include the Gardner D. Stout Hall of Asian Peoples, featuring displays of traditional costumes, furnishings, tools and musical instruments; the Hall of Mexico and Central America, with exhibits devoted to the Aztecs and Mayans; the Akeley Memorial Hall of African Mammals, with replicas of giant elephants; and, one of the newest exhibits, the Margaret Mead Hall of Pacific Peoples. The museum is famous for its fabulous collection of gems and crystals. The focal point of the Harry Frank Guggenheim Hall of Minerals is the spectacular 563-carat Star of India, the world's largest sapphire and the subject of a daring robbery in the 1970s that featured the notorious "Murph the Surf." (Also see "Major Attractions for Children" for the Hayden Planetarium and the Naturemax Theatre in the museum.)

1775 parlor

Brooklyn Museum

This graceful Beaux-Arts building, a short subway ride from midtown Manhattan, is home to a vast Egyptian collection that vies with—and in some ways even outdoes—the Metropolitan Museum of Art in its scope and richness. Of special note are its unparalleled Egyptian research library, the treasures from the tombs and vaults of Egypt's Old Kingdom, gorgeously stylized portrait-busts and beautiful green faience. The Brooklyn Museum's American galleries contain paintings by John Singer Sargent and Albert Pinkham Ryder as well as one version of Edward Hicks's "The Peaceable Kingdom." It also has charming period rooms, including a quaint two-room Dutch farmhouse and a Southern plantation. The magnificent sculptures in the recently installed Iris and Gerald Cantor Gallery include a statue from Rodin's celebrated "Burghers of Calais." Also worth seeing are the museum's Oriental and Middle Eastern art galleries and its textiles, costumes and decorative arts collections.

Museum of the City of New York

The history of the city of New York dating all the way back to the time of the Indians has been housed since the 1930s in this magnificent neo-Georgian mansion on Upper Fifth Avenue. The museum was originally located in Gracie Mansion, now the official residence of the mayor of New York City. The life and times of New York City are depicted in the museum's permanent and changing exhibitions of paintings, drawings, photographs, costumes, maps, prints, children's toys and dolls' houses, silver, porcelains and period rooms. The museum is famous for its excellent collection of theater memorabilia and its delightful rotating exhibits on New York City neighborhoods. Noteworthy exhibitions also include models and exhibits relating the early history of New York City, a Gilbert Stuart painting of George Washington, examples of Duncan Phyfe furniture, a collection of paintings and furniture that once belonged to Alexander Hamilton and architectural renderings of a number of famous Big Apple landmark buildings.

American Craft Museum

The American Craft Museum, which until 1979 was known as the Museum of Contemporary Crafts, was founded by New York state philanthropist Aileen Osborn Webb, who was herself an accomplished potter and woodcarver. For more than 35 years the museum has served as America's premier crafts showcase. Although it stages shows highlighting foreign artists, its emphasis is on American craftspeople. Its exhibits spotlight a wide variety of crafts, ranging from quilts and hand-fashioned jewelry to post-pop home design and works made of natural materials. The museum has even featured food as sculpture in several shows, including a popular exhibit of several seasons ago on chocolate sculpture. Since 1986 the American Craft Museum has been housed in a striking building on West 53rd Street near the Museum of Modern Art. Its huge glass window facade tempts passersby with a multilevel advance view of the exhibits. Inside, a 40-foot stair-atrium forms a dramatic backdrop for large-scale crafts objects.

Cooper-Hewitt Museum

The Cooper-Hewitt Museum is the Smithsonian Institution's National Museum of Design. For years the museum was located downtown at Cooper Union, a school noted for its departments of art and architecture, but in 1976 it moved to a magnificent 64-room mansion on Upper Fifth Avenue. The neo-Georgian house was built between 1899 and 1903 for millionaire industrialist and philanthropist Andrew Carnegie in an area of Manhattan that came to be known as Carnegie Hill. The building, with gorgeous carved woodwork, is a design achievement in itself and is on the National Register of Historic Places. The museum houses the world's most important and most extensive collection of design and decorative-arts objects, representing more than 3,000 years of design history. The collection of more than 300,000 objects includes ceramics, glass, prints, printed textiles, lace, embroidery, wrought iron, silverware, wall coverings, metalwork, woodwork, and European and American furniture. The library contains more than 40,000 books, and the museum's collection of architectural prints and design drawings is the world's largest. The Cooper-Hewitt's changing exhibits highlight historical and modern design and architecture.

The American Museum of the Moving Image

The American Museum of the Moving Image

Although Hollywood is America's movie capital today, the filmmaking industry actually started on the East Coast. One of the most important studios in the 1920s was the Astoria Studios, in Astoria, Queens, where the American Museum of the Moving Image stands today. Gloria Swanson, Rudolph Valentino, the Marx Brothers and a host of others all did their star turns here. With the recent revival of made-in-New York films, the Astoria Studios has leaped back into action. "Superman," "The Cotton Club" and Woody Allen's "Manhattan" are just a few of the movies made here in recent years.

An absolute must for film buffs, the museum houses exhibits on early movie-making equipment, costumes worn by the stars and a movie set from "The Glass Menagerie." Also shown are several movie theaters, including one called Tut's Fever, designed in the pseudo-Egyptian style of movie palaces in vogue in the 1930s. Highlights also include an 1894 Edison Kinetoscope, a 1927 Bell Laboratories large-screen television receiver and an 1895 movie-making machine created by the French movie-pioneering Lumière brothers.

Museum of Television and Radio

Formerly called the Museum of Broadcasting, this is a real treasure trove for enthusiasts of old-time television and radio. The museum's collection of 40,000 items includes thousands of radio and television programs dating from the 1920s. The shows in the collection include programs from the commercial stations as well as the public networks and a sampling of foreign broadcasts. The museum, which was founded in 1975 by William S. Paley, has just moved to a new home on 52nd Street, thus expanding its viewing and listening facilities. It now has a 200-seat theater, a 90-seat theater and two 45-seat screening rooms, which are used for its special presentations, talks by radio and TV luminaries, and regular viewings of the television shows in its archives. It also has a special radio listening room. You can also go off by yourself to listen to vintage broadcasts or watch old "I Love Lucy" episodes, Fred Astaire specials, Edward R. Murrow World War II broadcasts, newsreels, documentaries and TV commercials on one of the museum's video consoles. Once or twice a year the museum stages a blockbuster retrospective on a famous personality, which packs in the devotees.

Pierpont Morgan Library

Once the private library of financier J. Pierpont Morgan, today this gracious townhouse in Manhattan's Murray Hill district houses one of the most comprehensive collections of medieval and Renaissance manuscripts in the United States. The original wing of the library opened in 1906, when Morgan's passion for collecting forced him to find a repository for all his treasures. During his extensive travels he acquired early printed books, bookbindings, and old manuscripts and drawings, as well as architectural fragments from old European churches and cathedrals, some of which have been incorporated in the windows of the West Room. His collection of musical autographs, which includes works by Beethoven, Mahler, Mozart and Stravinsky, is second only to the one in the Library of Congress. The Morgan's Gilbert and Sullivan archive is the largest in the world. The museum has several charming period rooms, two of which have been preserved virtually intact from Morgan's day. The West Room, where he worked several hours every day, still contains his custom-made desk, and his portrait hangs over the fireplace.

Fraunces Tavern Museum

The museum occupies the reconstructed 18th-century Fraunces Tavern, best known as the place where, in 1783, Gen. George Washington bade farewell to the officers who had served under him during the Revolutionary War. The original 1719 building was a residence for a wealthy New Yorker, Stephen DeLancey, and his family. In 1762 an enterprising West Indian, Samuel Fraunces, bought the three-story mansion and transformed it into a tavern. It quickly became a popular gathering place for leaders of the Revolution, including the Sons of Liberty and our future first president. During the brief period when New York City served as our nation's first capital, John Jay and other important government officials frequently met here. Fraunces Tavern opened to the public as a museum in 1907. Modern-day visitors can tour the Long Room, where Washington held his farewell address, see an audiovisual on the tavern and the history of early New York, and explore the museum's collection of 18th-century arts and artifacts. Special celebrations are held on July Fourth and George Washington's birthday. The building, by the way, still houses a restaurant whose specialty is Chicken Washington.

Jewish Museum

America's largest collection of Judaica is housed in the former French Gothic residence of millionaire philanthropist Felix M. Warburg. The building is located on Upper Fifth Avenue's Museum Mile. The museum's permanent collection of approximately 15,000 objects includes a vast number of ceremonial religious items that span the ages and the continents. Artworks include paintings by Marc Chagall, Rembrandt and other artists as well as drawings, prints, sculptures, cultural artifacts, textiles and decorative-arts objects. Although many of the Jewish Museum's exhibitions focus on the fine arts, its changing exhibitions do not shy away from social commentary and controversy. Recent exhibits have explored the tense relationship between Soviet society and Russian Jews, the Dreyfus Affair and Jewish life in the European ghettoes. The Jewish Museum is currently in the midst of a major renovation, which will be completed in late 1992. Until then, its exhibitions are being shown at the New-York Historical Society.

Frick Collection

The superb art collection amassed by coke and steel magnate Henry Clay Frick is housed in this gorgeous 40-room townhouse located at Fifth Avenue and 70th Street. The museum, which is just around the corner from Central Park, is a great favorite of New Yorkers, probably because it still retains its residential decor and ambience. The Frick is famous for its excellent collection of 14th- to 19th-century European paintings. Its treasures include a Rembrandt self-portrait, Holbein's "Sir Thomas More," Ingres' "Comtesse d'Haussonville," Goya's portrait of the Duke of Osuna, and paintings by Titian, Reynolds, Turner, Van Dyck and Velasquez. There are several opulently furnished rooms with period wall-coverings, furniture and accessories. A commanding portrait of Frick himself hangs over the mantel in one of the period rooms. The museum is also known for its fine collections of Limoges china, enamelware, silver, porcelains and prints. A charming inner garden court adorned with fountains is the setting for chamber music concerts on certain Sundays.

Schomburg Center for Research in Black Culture

The Schomburg Center houses what is generally regarded as America's—and perhaps the world's—foremost collection of cultural and historical artifacts and material relating to the black experience in the United States, Africa and elsewhere. The Schomburg is located at Lenox Avenue and 135th Street in Harlem and is actually a branch of the New York Public Library. It was founded and named for a Puerto Rican, Arthur Schomburg. Writers, historians and students of black history come here to make use of its awesome research and exhibition facilities. Generations of Afro-American artists and writers such as James Baldwin have found a welcome home away from home at the Schomburg, whose holdings include about 75,000 books, 200,000 manuscripts, more than 20,000 reels of microfilm and 10,000 items on microfiche. The center has an excellent collection of paintings, sculpture, and arts and crafts by black Americans, as well as Afro-American cultural artifacts, maps, historical photographs, videotapes, recorded music, posters and playbills. The Schomburg frequently stages special exhibitions paying tribute to individuals and events that figured prominently in black history.

Lower East Side Tenement Museum

One of New York City's newest museums is housed in a former tenement building on Orchard Street on the Lower East Side. The building was the first home in America for literally thousands of new immigrants, starting from the 1860s up through the 1930s, when New York City instituted stricter building codes. Many of the people who resided in this and similar neighborhood buildings lived in tiny rooms in "shifts" with fellow immigrants. As one resident would get out of bed to go to work on the night shift, another would take his place after a hard day's work. The museum organizers are trying to trace descendants of former inhabitants in order to create recorded histories of their ancestors' early experiences here. In the meantime the museum holds regular living-history programs—usually on Sundays—and walking tours that re-create the lives of Poles, Ukrainians, Jews, Germans, Afro-Americans, Italians, Chinese and other immigrants. Recent programs included The Washingtons: Free Africans in 19th-Century New York and a Peddler's Pack Walking Tour, which traced the lives of an immigrant Jewish family through visits to schools, synagogues and former sweat shops.

Museum of the American Indian

The museum's 1.3 million art objects and cultural artifacts devoted to the Indians of North, Central and South America constitute the largest collection of its kind. The collection includes ethnographical and archaeological objects as well as ornamental and decorative items, household utensils, tools, ceremonial objects, weapons, and children's toys and dolls. Special highlights include Crazy Horse's feather headdress, kachina dolls made by the Hopi Indians, a cane and war cap that belonged to Geronimo, Amazon blow guns and garments worn by the Apaches. After years of controversy over what many critics regarded as the museum's inconvenient location (on Manhattan's Upper West Side near 155th Street), a compromise was worked out. In 1993 the museum, which is a part of the Smithsonian Institution, will take over 7,000 square feet of exhibition space in the former U.S. Customs House in Lower Manhattan, while the bulk of the collection will be stored in a facility in the Washington area (probably Virginia or Maryland). In 1998 the museum will add a second exhibition facility on the Mall in Washington.

Museum of American Folk Art

The museum, which was founded in 1961, is one of the country's leading institutions dedicated to the preservation and presentation of American folk art. The collection encompasses paintings, sculptures, crafts, furniture, ceramics and textiles that highlight various facets of our country's folk art from the Colonial period up to the present. The permanent collection displays such charming everyday objects as quilts, wooden musical instruments, samplers, hourglasses, weather vanes and handcrafted circus animals that were made to adorn carousels. Exhibitions devoted to a particular period or craft style are scheduled periodically. The Museum of American Folk Art is a co-sponsor of the prestigious Fall Antiques Show, which takes place every October at Pier 92 (Hudson River near West 55th Street). It is currently located in the Lincoln Center area, but sometime in 1992 or shortly thereafter it will move into new quarters next to the Museum of Modern Art. The museum, however, will continue to maintain the Lincoln Center location as a branch.

Broadway Theater

In spite of rising costs of both tickets and productions, the loss of audience to video rentals and TV, and the constant carping by critics that shows aren't what they used to be, New York City is still the theater capital of the world. In fact as far as the bottom line is concerned, show business is better than ever. The most recent tally by the League of American Theatres and Producers revealed that 8 million theatergoers spent $283 million in one season to see 35 new productions—a box office record.

The Broadway theater as we know it today has achieved its world-renowned status in less than 100 years. Of the area's 38 theaters, the oldest—the newly restored Victory on 42nd Street—opened in 1900 as Oscar Hammerstein's Theatre Republic. It was here, along Broadway between 39th and 40th streets, that the old (1883) Metropolitan Opera stood before it moved to its spacious new quarters in Lincoln Center in 1966. Although everyone agreed that the old Met was cramped and inefficient (sets often had to be stashed on the sidewalk out the back door between scene changes), the musty gold-and-red-plush interior had the look and feel of a proper Old World opera house and it was passionately loved by the fans. Its demolition—and the later razing of two other historic Broadway-area theaters, the Morosco and the Helen Hayes—caused such protest that the city's landmarking laws were extended to other notable structures. Now protected are the 1903 Lyceum, the 1907 Belasco and the 1913 Shubert (recently the home of Broadway's longest-running show, "A Chorus Line," which played 6,137 performances).

Even in profitable times, not all of Broadway's 38 theaters will be occupied at the same time, but theatergoers can count on finding at least 15 to 20 shows running in any season. Fall, winter and spring are the hottest times on Broadway; these are the months when most of the new shows open. Following the annual Tony Awards in June—an event that signals the end of a current season—the summer tourist season sets in. Millions of visitors from all over the world come to see the hits that have garnered the most prizes, have been blessed by the influential critics and—perhaps most important—have been touted by word of mouth.

Musicals continue to be the most popular Broadway shows, followed by comedies and dramas. Spectacles such as "Miss Saigon," "The Phantom of the Opera," "Les Miserables," "Cats" and "Fiddler on the Roof" pack the houses night after night, whereas works by Shakespeare, Molière or even 20th-century dramatists with the stature of Eugene O'Neill, Arthur Miller or Tennessee Williams won't be produced without a major star to attract the crowds.

To help you decide what shows to see, read as much as you can about the current offerings and keep your ears open for all the Broadway gossip—it's great fun. But never let negative comments about certain shows or the state of the theater put you off from seeing something that sparks your interests. Critics and other doomsayers have been burying the theater since the first production was staged.

What is the best way to get tickets? If you absolutely must see the hottest shows in town, you should obtain tickets as far in advance as possible by (1) checking a listing in a national newspaper or magazine and writing the theater for an order form, (2) charging tickets via phone on a credit card, either at the theater box office or through a ticket service such as Ticketron or (3) obtaining your tickets through a ticket broker. Whatever route you take, be prepared to pay additional service charges—all legitimate—above the ticket price.

If you simply want the experience of attending a top-flight show—without all the bother of advance arrangements and without tying yourself down to an inflexible schedule— check in at the TKTS half-price ticket booths. An uptown booth, outdoors, is at 47th and Broadway, and an indoor downtown booth is at World Trade Center Tower 2 on the mezzanine level. Some 30 shows, on- and off-Broadway, are offered at half price (plus a $2 per ticket service charge) on the day of performance only. The downtown booth will also offer a selection of matinee tickets a day in advance. Even London hits, critics' favorites or shows from established hit-makers like Neil Simon will start offering tickets at the TKTS booths within months—often weeks—of opening. Seats are never in prime, fifth-row-center locations, but all are full-view, perfectly good seats; sometimes, during slack periods or on off nights, the locations can be excellent. Remember, you could be getting a $60 seat for $30 plus $2, a considerable saving. The best seats and the widest choices are available during weekdays and for matinees, since Friday and Saturday evenings are the most popular nights at the theater.

Another budget-saving device for theater tickets is the use of "twofers," those coupons that can be exchanged at theater box offices for reduced-price tickets. The tickets are not half price, but the seats are a bit better and you can purchase tickets for advance dates as well as day of performance. Twofers are available at the Visitors and Convention Bureau (2 Columbus Circle), at hotels and at other locations around town.

What if the shows you want are not listed at the TKTS booths? You can always try the box offices for full-price seats or go one to two hours before curtain time and join the line for last-minute cancellations. This last method is often the only way to get into the biggest hits. Still another ticket source is your hotel's concierge, who often has an "in" with theater box offices. As for black-market tickets . . . all those who love the theater deplore the practice of using scalpers. The prices are exorbitant, the tickets often bogus and the excessive cost involved never goes to either performers or producers.

When attending theater performances, give yourself plenty of time and arrive well before curtain rise (almost always at 8 o'clock for evening performances, 2 or 3 o'clock for matinees), especially if you have to pick up prearranged, charged tickets. Use the extra time to admire the theater's architecture and interior design; historic houses like the Belasco, Lyceum, Martin Beck, Music Box and Majestic are treasure houses of stained glass, carved marble, mosaics, sculptures, and ornamental plasterwork. Once settled in your seat, read the Playbill feature on the history of the theater you're attending. You'll learn about all the famous plays and performers that have graced these stages through the years.

Joseph Papp's Public Theater

Off- and Off-Off-Broadway

Although its houses are small—some have fewer than 100 seats—the off- and off-off-Broadway area is by far the largest and most active part of New York City's theater scene. Many theatergoers and critics think it's the most creative part.

Off-Broadway is by no means second-class quality. The theater's top writers—among them Eugene O'Neill, Arthur Miller, Tennessee Williams, Lanford Wilson, Edward Albee, Beth Henley, Caryl Churchill, Wendy Wasserstein, Stephen Sondheim and Harvey Fierstein—have had some of their greatest triumphs a world away from the bright lights of Times Square. Sam Shepard, one of America's most influential playwrights, has never had a Broadway production.

As an innovator, off-Broadway has had an increasingly strong influence on Broadway ever since the post–World War I days when small playhouses in Greenwich Village gave a voice to such budding writers as e.e. cummings, Paul Green, Sherwood Anderson, Theodore Dreiser, Edna Ferber, Edna St. Vincent Millay and the early Eugene O'Neill. The Provincetown Playhouse on MacDougal Street below Washington Square and the Cherry Lane on

Commerce Street are among these small theaters that are still operating today. It was at the Provincetown that O'Neill's one-act plays were first produced, where his "Emperor Jones" with Charles Gilpin was first staged, and where Paul Robeson made his debut in O'Neill's "All God's Chillun Got Wings."

"Steel Magnolias" at the WPA Theater

In the 1920s and '30s off-Broadway continued to serve as the theater's avant-garde arm—an outlet for creative talent that the commercial, uptown theater wouldn't gamble on. After World War II such revivals as Eugene O'Neill's "The Iceman Cometh" and Tennessee Williams' "Summer and Smoke," both of which were presented by the Circle in the Square, enjoyed critical and popular success. Thus off-Broadway proved it could satisfy a cultural hunger ignored by the big theaters.

Off-Broadway became a proving ground for the Broadway stage. "Hair," "Big River," "The Fifth of July," "Talley's Folly," Stephen Sondheim's "Sunday in the Park with George," "Ain't Misbehavin'" and Harvey Fierstein's "Torch Song Trilogy"—all began off-Broadway before moving to Times Square for long runs. "A Chorus Line," Broadway's longest-running show ever, began as a workshop production in Joseph Papp's Public Theater in the downtown NoHo area.

Today there are more than 300 off- and off-off-Broadway theaters in all five boroughs of the city. These venues range from abandoned garages to school assembly halls, lofts and store fronts, bars and churches. Not all of them are in use at any one time, but theatergoers can count on at least 100 choices even in slack periods.

Off-Broadway differs from Broadway in more ways than size and a willingness to be more experimental. Because all off-Broadway houses have fewer than 300 seats (some are as small as 50!), costs, both for productions and for actors, are kept to a minimum. Under an agreement with Actors Equity, the stage actors' union, plays can be given "showcase" productions for a limited run with salaries considerably below Broadway scale. Generally the limited-run theaters are the off-off-Broadway houses. If a show

succeeds with critics and the public, it can consider a move to off-Broadway status, where it can have an open run. This means a contract for the actors' salaries and a higher ticket price—although in both cases still much lower than Broadway rates. Another option for an off-off-Broadway success is a direct move to Broadway, although more and more hit shows elect to stay off-Broadway where they won't have to fight the stresses and expenses of a Broadway move. Recent examples of shows that settled into long and profitable off-Broadway runs are "Forbidden Broadway," "Nunsense" and "Perfect Crime." Other off-Broadway successes—such as "Driving Miss Daisy," "Steel Magnolias," "Little Shop of Horrors" and "The Boys in the Band"—went directly to Hollywood.

Some of the best-known off-Broadway theaters are Joseph Papp's Public Theater (actually six theaters in the old Astor Library), the Circle Repertory Theater, the Manhattan Theatre Club, Playwrights Horizon, La Mama, American Place Theater, Ensemble Studio Theater, the WPA Theater and the Oasis Theatre Company (one of the newer groups). Off- and off-off-Broadway theaters are located through the city, but concentrations are found in Greenwich Village, along Theater Row on West 42nd Street, on the Upper West Side (both west and north of the Broadway theatre district), in Chelsea and on the Upper East Side.

Carnegie Hall

On May 5, 1891, the composer Peter Ilich Tchaikovsky conducted his own works at the opening of the massive new auditorium at 57th Street and Seventh Avenue. Since then musicians and music lovers everywhere have called Carnegie Hall "the world's favorite concert hall."

Although anyone can tour this hallowed temple of the arts and anyone can buy a seat to a performance, only the finest artists can grace its pristine, cream-and-gold, classically arched stage. The greatest names in classical music—Mahler, Richard Strauss, Bernstein, Horowitz, and the world's leading orchestras and soloists—have played to packed houses that have sold out in a matter of hours. Opera, too, plays a prominent role in the Carnegie Hall schedule—in recital performances of works neglected by the big opera houses.

Jazz and pop have also contributed some of the hall's most memorable moments. Prominent lecturers, distinguished speakers and worthy causes have occupied the Carnegie stage.

New York almost lost Carnegie Hall to the wrecking ball back in the 1960s, when yet another skyscraper was to take its place. An enraged public led by the redoubtable Isaac Stern—who is now Carnegie's president—won the battle for culture vultures everywhere. Instead of being demolished, the venerable hall was given a top-to-bottom, $50 million restoration and renovation that enlarged the stage and lobby areas, put in new seats and elevators, replaced wiring and air-conditioning ducts and improved sight lines in the box-seat sections—while preserving the hall's excellent acoustics.

Carnegie Hall is also much more than its incomparable auditorium. To the left of the main entrance is the Joan and Sanford I. Weill Recital Hall, a jewel box where fledgling singers, pianists and other instrumentalists test their musical wings. In the basement along the Seventh Avenue side is the Carnegie Hall Cinema, where first-run, usually avant-garde films are screened. Upstairs in the tower sections is a complex of studios, apartments, recital halls, classrooms and workshop theater space.

Town Hall

A handsome, Georgian-style auditorium located in the Broadway and Times Square area at 123 W. 43rd St., Town Hall opened in 1921 as a civic concert hall. The theater seats 1,498 and boasts excellent acoustics.

In the past Town Hall has been the scene of concerts, recitals (Joan Sutherland's New York City debut was held here), musicals, tributes and lectures. Winston Churchill, Eleanor Roosevelt, William Butler Yeats, Richard Nixon and Margaret Sanger spoke here. Singers, musicians and composers who have performed here include Sergei Rachmaninoff, Pablo Casals, Jan Peerce, Marian Anderson, Richard Tucker, Duke Ellington and Miles Davis.

Town Hall has an eclectic schedule of special events. Recent offerings have included a jazz festival and several cabaret conventions starring today's leading lounge singers.

In 1990 Town Hall began an ambitious, 10-year, decade-by-decade look at the arts and social history of 20th-century New York. Titled Century of Change, the survey consists of five programs each year through 1999 devoted to the music, art, literature, politics and technology of each decade.

City Center

It looks like a Moorish temple—something out of the Arabian Nights—and no wonder: It was built in 1924 as the Masonic Mecca Temple for the Ancient and Accepted Order of the Mystic Shrine, better known as the Shriners. It was used for the next 20 years as the Shriners' lodge, banquet hall and auditorium.

A financial burden to the Shriners from the beginning, the temple was eventually repossessed by the city government, and in 1944 it was converted into City Center Theater by Mayor Fiorello La Guardia. Both the New York City Opera and the New York City Ballet had their first homes here before moving to Lincoln Center, and early performers included such legends as ballet star Maria Tallchief and opera diva Beverly Sills.

Critics have made fun of City Center's extravagant architecture, but it has become a much-beloved city landmark and was restored and renovated in 1980. Today the building's sandstone facade glows, the glazed ceramic tile mosaics gleam and the brass entrances are kept highly polished. The redesign of the foyer and orchestra level seating improved sight lines. Another thrill of restoration was the uncovering of the brilliantly colored mural on the ceiling of the mezzanine lobby—a dazzling pattern of gold, blue and burgundy arabesques that had been hidden by paint for 20 years.

As one of the world's leading showcases for both classical and modern ballet, the 2,734-seat City Center has presented such acclaimed groups as the Martha Graham Dance Company, the Alvin Ailey American Dance Theater, the Trisha Brown and Merce Cunningham Dance Companies and the Georgian State Dance Company from the Caucasus in the U.S.S.R.

Brooklyn Academy of Music (BAM)

This 1905 temple of performing arts is located in the heart of Brooklyn at 30 Lafayette Ave., only 20 minutes away from Times Square by express subway. Some of the city's most critically acclaimed productions and performers are presented only at BAM. In addition, many hit Broadway productions opened first at BAM before moving to Manhattan.

A white, glazed-brick building with terra cotta ornamentation and sculptures, BAM is actually several performing spaces in one massive building. Off the spacious lobby, which runs the length of the building, are several auditoriums. The 2,100-seat Opera House is an auditorium in the grand, Old World style, with majestic boxes. The Helen Carey Playhouse has 1,078 seats, and the small Attic Theater has only 199 seats. The 750-seat Lepercq Space can be adapted to theater or dance via bleacher seating.

Although the present building dates from the early 20th century, BAM was founded in 1859, making it, according to some accounts, the oldest music center in the nation. In its early years it was one of the leading stops on the theatrical circuit, and among the famous performers to grace its stages were Enrico Caruso, the noted tenor; Sarah Bernhardt, who appeared in "Camille"; Anna Pavlova, the legendary dancer, who performed such classics as "The Dying Swan"; and Edwin Booth, who presented his incomparable Hamlet. In recent years BAM has concentrated chiefly on avant-garde or seldom-produced works.

Metropolitan Opera House

Lincoln Center for the Performing Arts

Stretching four blocks—between 62nd and 66th streets, between Broadway and Amsterdam Avenue on Manhattan's Upper West Side, Lincoln Center for the Performing Arts is the world's largest and most influential cultural complex. Opera, classical music, dance, theater and film—all are celebrated in this eight-building center, which cost $165 million when it was built back in the 1960s. Most of the funds came from private contributions.

Each building has a distinct personality while at the same time contributing to the unity of the center. The center's three largest buildings—Avery Fisher Hall, the New York State Theater and the Metropolitan Opera—form three sides of a quadrangle facing Broadway. In the center of the quadrangle's spacious plaza is a circular fountain that is a

favorite meeting place. In summer there is a sidewalk cafe and ice cream stands and in winter a delightful Christmas tree decorated with lights in the shape of musical instruments.

Avery Fisher Hall, the home of the New York Philharmonic and other classical groups, was the first house to be completed. It is a five-story, clear-glass rectangle set inside an arcade defined by travertine columns. It is particularly spectacular at night when the multitiered lobbies that surround the auditorium are brightly illuminated. The 2,738-seat concert hall itself is a rather spare, minimalist interior in shades of white and gold, set off by a soaring stage faced with light-colored wood paneling. Richard Lippold's sculpture "Orpheus and Apollo," a shiny splash of 190 polished metal strips, is suspended from the ceiling of the hall's vast promenade by stainless steel wires.

The New York State Theater, designed by Philip Johnson (who also did the plaza fountain), is the home of the New York City Opera and the New York City Ballet. A glittering jewel box with gold-leaf ceilings, carpeted walls, red plush seats and carpeting, diamond-shaped lights and bronze railings, the 2,737-seat theater is considered by many visitors and critics alike the most successful, the most comfortable house in Lincoln Center. The spacious entrance lobby is flanked by dramatic staircases at either end leading up to the orchestra level lobby, another spacious area that serves as an atrium reaching to the top-level balcony area. Balconies on each level completely surround this soaring atrium, inviting patrons of the upper levels to promenade during intermission periods.

The huge Metropolitan Opera House—3,718 seats—was the last of the center's main buildings to be completed in 1966. A grande dame in every way, the Met is the epitome of opulence. The facade, a glass front formed by five colonnaded arches, is a dazzling sight, especially at night. Two giant Chagall murals, blazing with color and peopled with operatic characters, fill up the two outside arches. A huge Austrian cut-glass chandelier glitters through the center arch. Outside and inside balconies on the Met's various levels permit patrons to observe the center's active plaza scene during intermissions.

Countries throughout the world contributed to the Met's furnishings. West Germany (now a part of Germany) bestowed the enormous and mechanically complex stage. The walls of the interior are covered with African rosewood veneer that comes from one single log, and all of the chandeliers—star bursts of myriad crystal prisms—were donated by Austria.

Theatrical productions are held in the large (1,140 seats) Vivian Beaumont Theater and the smaller (299 seats) Mitzi E. Newhouse Theater. Just outside the theater building is a large, rectangular reflecting pool containing Henry Moore's enormous bronze sculpture "Reclining Figure." To the left of the theater building is the invaluable Library & Museum of the Performing Arts, where you can listen to classical recordings, check the stars of a play or do research on grand opera. Behind and to the north of this pool are the center's other buildings, the Juilliard School and Alice Tully Hall. The Juilliard School has a large, beautiful auditorium where highly polished student concerts, operas and ballets are presented. Alice Tully Hall plays host to the Chamber Music Society, the annual New York Film Festival, pop stars and recital artists.

Above: Quadrangle of Lincoln Center
Right: The New York Philharmonic at Alice Tully Hall

Richmondtown Restoration

Staten Island—the smallest, greenest and most rustic of New York's five boroughs—is the home of one of the city's most extensive historic sites. A historic village containing 26 buildings dating from the 17th through the 19th centuries, Richmondtown covers 96 acres in Staten Island's Greenbelt area. Eleven of the buildings are on their original sites. Interiors on display include the 1695 Voorlezer's House, which is the country's oldest elementary schoolhouse still standing; the Stephens House and General Store; the 1770 Boehm House, which contains an exhibit on historic preservation and restoration techniques; the Basketmaker's House; the Bennett House, with its display of dolls and toys; and the Richmondtown Historical Museum.

Guided tours are available all year, or visitors can stroll around on their own, surrendering to the peaceful atmosphere of another time. You can observe demonstrations of leather working, pottery making, tinsmithing, printing, carpentry, spinning and weaving, basketmaking and open-hearth cooking. An attractive gift shop offers books, historical souvenirs and authentic reproductions. Special events and workshops are held throughout the year, and the Christmas in Richmondtown celebrations are extremely popular.

Richmondtown Historical Museum

General Grant National Memorial

To the corny old question "Who's buried in Grant's Tomb?" the proper answer is President and Mrs. Grant. As you will see when you enter the 1897 monumental mausoleum, the remains of Ulysses S. Grant and his wife, Julia Dent Grant, are entombed side by side in twin polished black sarcophagi.

Situated on a bluff overlooking the Hudson River at Riverside Drive and 122nd Street, the 150-foot-high white granite memorial is said to be a free copy of the ancient tomb of Governor Mausoleus at Halicarnassus in present-day Turkey. It has also been compared, in size and pretentiousness, with Napoleon's tomb in Paris, and it still holds the record as the largest mausoleum in America.

You enter the tomb through a square Ionic temple with six fluted columns. Then you pass through massive bronze doors into a white marble rotunda overlooking the sunken, open crypt. Four carved figures in the rotunda represent the four stages in the general's life: youth, the military, civil life and death. In the north end of the tomb are rooms displaying Grant memorabilia, and outside, over the tomb's entrance, are inscribed the general's famous words: "Let there be peace."

Theodore Roosevelt's Birthplace

The impressive, beautifully cared for townhouse at 28 E. 20th St. in the Gramercy Park district marks the birthplace of Theodore Roosevelt in 1858. The nation's 26th president and the only president born in New York City, he lived here until he was 15 years old. Although the original 1848 brownstone was demolished, it was lovingly reproduced in 1923 by the Theodore Roosevelt Association. The period furnishings faithfully re-create the upper-class Victorian lifestyle of young Teddy and his family. Most of the furniture was donated by the Roosevelts, and it includes a rather severe horsehair sofa, which must not have encouraged guests to linger at tea.

A National Historic Site, the Theodore Roosevelt birthplace is a museum as well as a restored home. The displayed memorabilia from the president's eventful life is extensive. It includes items and papers from his days as a Dakota Territory rancher, a colonel in the Rough Riders and vice president under William McKinley and from his lifelong interest as a naturalist.

Edgar Allan Poe's Cottage

Poe's last home (1846–49) is a sunny, cheerful, 1812 cottage set in the middle of a small park in the Bronx. The two-story house, now located in Poe Park at Grand Concourse and East Kingsbridge Road, was moved here in 1913 from its original site across the road.

Today it seems impossible to believe that so much suffering went on in this pleasant place. Poe was near the end of his rope. His beloved child bride, Virginia, died of consumption here; her mother, Mrs. Maria Clemm, lived with them, and all three existed on the edge of starvation. This is where Poe wrote "Ulalume," "The Bells" and "Annabel Lee."

Always a restless soul, Poe had lived in houses down in Greenwich Village and on Manhattan's Upper West Side, but he came to this cottage in what was then the country, hoping the restful atmosphere and fresh air would cure his wife's tuberculosis. Her death in 1847 was followed two years later by his own. On his way back to the cottage from a trip to Virginia, he died en route in Baltimore.

Gracie Mansion

The official home of New York's mayors since 1942 (Fiorello La Guardia's administration), Gracie Mansion was built by Archibald Gracie in 1799 as a country house on the banks of the East River. Located today in what is now called Carl Schurz Park at the end of East 88th Street, the mansion—beautifully restored and expanded—is open to individuals and groups by appointment only.

As the sole survivor of its type and period, Gracie Mansion gives visitors an excellent feeling for the life of a late-18th-century landowner. The front parlors, furnished with period pieces, are large and airy with high ceilings, and they overlook a wide porch that faces the East River, Ward's and Randall's islands, and the huge Triborough Bridge. A spacious lawn bordered by flower beds sweeps down to a railing overlooking the water.

Morris-Jumel Mansion

Looking somewhat like Tara in "Gone With the Wind" and commanding one of the finest views in Manhattan, the Morris-Jumel Mansion stands in Harlem on a hill at 161st Street and Edgecombe Avenue. It is set amid landscaped grounds and gardens that enhance its beauty. Built in 1765—with later additions—in Georgian-Federal style, the mansion has had a rich and varied past. First it was the country estate of Roger Morris, a loyalist to the Crown. In the early stages of the Revolutionary War, during the Battle of Harlem Heights, it served as Gen. George Washington's headquarters. When that campaign was lost the house fell into British hands until the war's end. It then served as a tavern until 1810, when Stephen Jumel, a French wine merchant, purchased it for his wife Eliza, who restored the mansion to its former glory and furnished it in Empire style. After Jumel's death in 1832 Aaron Burr, third vice president of the United States, married Mme. Jumel and lived here.

Tours of the house—which is elegantly furnished with period pieces, many of which belonged to the various occupants—are conducted by the Daughters of the American Revolution, who preside over this historic landmark.

Bowne House

A modest Colonial house built in 1661 in what is now the borough of Queens, Bowne House is one of the nation's most important shrines to religious freedom.

Peter Stuyvesant, governor of New Amsterdam (New York's name before the British took over in 1664), outlawed the Society of Friends when he took office in the mid-17th century. Because all meetings of the Quakers were forbidden, the society first met clandestinely in the woods and then in this house, which John Bowne built on land he bought from the Indians for eight strings of white wampum—or so the story goes.

A two-story house with a steep pitched roof, dormer windows and a small Dutch entranceway porch, the Bowne House is the oldest house in Queens and one of the oldest in New York state. It was dedicated as a National Shrine on October 10, 1945. The furnishings include a bed slept in by William Penn on a 1700 visit; a sofa sat upon by William Fox, founder of the Society of Friends; and a walking stick John Bowne used to kill a bear.

2 and 3 Pierrepont Place

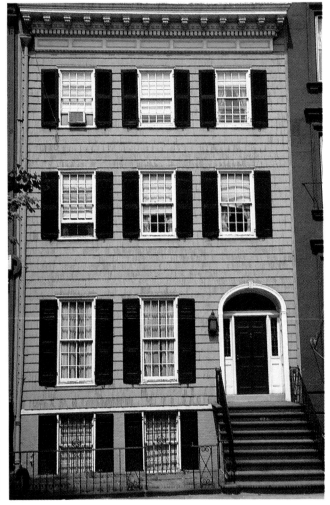

Brooklyn Heights Historic District

In a city built for strolling, Brooklyn Heights offers some of the most delightful walking-tour possibilities in all the five boroughs. The first stop in Brooklyn Heights should be The Esplanade, or Promenade, as it is known locally, which overlooks New York Harbor and the Manhattan skyline. It is one of the city's most spectacular views, one that includes the Statue of Liberty, Ellis Island and the Governor's Island Coast Guard Station. Flanking The Esplanade and facing the view is a long row of handsome townhouses with entrances on Columbia Heights, the first street paralleling the promenade. Leading off Columbia Heights are such streets as Remsen, Montague, Pierrepont, Clark, Pineapple, Orange, Cranberry and Middagh—each one of them a treasure of 19th-century houses, apartments, churches, clubs and historic buildings. Two examples are the 1878 Long Island Historical Society at 128 Pierrepont and the original headquarters (1857–1895) of the Brooklyn Union Gas company at 180 Remsen St.

Although the area is small and compact, it would take a week or more to soak up all the riches of the area. Three houses, however, are especially interesting. One is an 1824 Federal house with garden cottage at 24 Middagh St., which is the oldest house. The other two are townhouses at 2 and 3 Pierrepont Place and have been called the most elegant brownstones left in New York.

Hamilton Grange National Memorial

The country home of Alexander Hamilton, the first U.S. Secretary of the Treasury, is a Federal-style frame house built in 1802. The Hamilton Grange originally stood two blocks farther north from its present location in Harlem at 287 Convent Ave. Here it is squeezed in between St. Luke's Church and an apartment complex.

For decades plans have been made to move the house yet again to a more fitting location, but more pressing problems intervene. In the meantime, Hamilton Grange is included on most guided tours of the Harlem area. Unfortunately the house furnishings are sparse because of lack of funding, and visitors must imagine what the Grange looked like when it was home to one of the nation's most important historic figures.

The entire area, now designated the Hamilton Heights Historic District, was once part of Hamilton's country estate. Now containing attractive row houses dating from the turn of the century, the neighborhood primarily serves as living quarters for faculty and administrators from nearby City College.

Wave Hill

The history of Wave Hill—an 1843 Georgian mansion on a 28-acre estate in the Bronx, overlooking the Hudson River—is filled with famous names. Mark Twain, Theodore Roosevelt and Arturo Toscanini lived here, and famous guests included William Makepeace Thackeray, T.H. Huxley and Herbert Spencer. For a while, it was the official residence of the United Kingdom's United Nations ambassador. When you see the glorious river views and the elaborate gardens, you'll understand why this dramatic setting has attracted so much attention—and so many notables—over the years.

Wave Hill's buildings—the original center section and the wings added in the late 19th and early 20th centuries—were given to the city in 1960. Today they are the home of the Wave Hill Center for Environmental Studies and the City University of New York Institute of Marine and Atmospheric Sciences at City College. The gardens contain thousands of floral specimens in wild and formal gardens and in greenhouses. Now the gardens are planted with sculptures as well as flowers. Wave Hill's exhibit areas offer frequent art shows and musical and dance performances.

Castle Clinton National Monument

An imposing circular stone structure in Battery Park at the tip of Lower Manhattan, Castle Clinton was built as a fort to protect New York Harbor during the War of 1812. (Its twin, Castle Williams, stands on Governor's Island, now a Coast Guard station.) Luckily, the forts never saw military action, and Castle Clinton is in mint condition—one of the oldest historic sites in a city where few sites have escaped the onslaught of progress.

The old fort, hand-tooled out of brownstone, has had a varied history. As a national monument it received the early city's distinguished visitors. From 1823 to 1855 the vastly remodeled fort—called Castle Garden—served as a concert hall. Its most famous guest star was Jenny Lind, the "Swedish Nightingale," who made her American debut here in 1850. Five years later the concert hall was transformed into the city's Immigrant Landing Depot, where almost 7.7 million new Americans were processed over the years. With the opening of the Ellis Island immigrant station in 1892, the old fort became the city's aquarium (1896–1941).

In 1976 Castle Clinton was restored to its original appearance. It contains exhibits showing what army life was like in the nation's early history, and it also has a small museum of artifacts from the fort's life as an immigrant depot. This is also the place where tickets are bought for the ferry that takes you to the Statue of Liberty and Ellis Island.

Federal Hall National Memorial

Many visitors either don't know or tend to forget that New York was the nation's first capital. The modern city has so overwhelmed its historic sites that it seems impossible that cobblestone streets and Colonial houses once stood where we find the sunless canyons with skyscraper walls that make up the Wall Street financial district today.

The old Federal Hall, where George Washington took the oath of office as first president on April 30, 1789, was demolished in the early 19th century. The handsome Greek revival building that now stands on the site at Wall and Nassau streets was built in 1842 as a U.S. Customs House, which was converted into the U.S. Subtreasury. The vaults are still visible in the corners of the beautiful rotunda room.

Federal Hall National Memorial is a museum honoring George Washington, the United States presidency and the concept of freedom of speech. The landmark freedom of the press trial of newspaperman John Peter Zenger was held in the old Federal Hall. On August 4, 1775, he was acquitted of "false, scandalous, malicious and seditious libel" against New York's Royal Governor. A famous statue of President Washington by J.Q.A. Ward stands on the front steps of the museum.

Trinity Church

The tall Gothic spire of Trinity Church stands on lower Broadway facing down the Wall Street canyon, which runs west to east. Trinity was chartered in 1696 as the first Anglican parish in New York. Because the original church building was burned during the American Revolution, George Washington worshiped at St. Paul's Chapel a few blocks north following his 1789 inaugural. (Built in 1766, St. Paul's is the only pre–Revolutionary War public building left standing in New York, and among the treasures in its lovely interior is Washington's pew.) The present structure was completed in 1846.

A large, impressive church with a thriving congregation, Trinity Church contains a small museum displaying early church documents and artifacts. The church is noted for its altar and choir screen. The green, tombstone-studded churchyard, a favorite retreat for financial-district office workers, contains the graves and memorials of such famous New Yorkers as Alexander Hamilton, Robert Fulton and Capt. James Lawrence, the War of 1812 hero who uttered the words, "Don't give up the ship!"

Flatiron Building and Ladies' Mile District

From the mid-19th century to the early 20th century, New York's premier shopping district, called "Ladies' Mile," was located in an area roughly marked by Union Square on the south, Madison Square on the north, Park Avenue South on the east and Sixth Avenue on the west. Here, in grand, cast-iron and marble-trimmed buildings of Beaux Arts architecture, were located such famous emporiums as Arnold Constable, B. Altman, F.A.O. Schwarz, Gorham, Hugh O'Neill Dry Goods, Lord & Taylor and W. & J. Sloane.

In the heyday of Ladies' Mile shoppers arrived and departed by horse-drawn carriage and on fine days promenaded along the avenues from one store to another. Many of the fabulous buildings they visited are still standing; the area is now a protected landmark. One of the most interesting buildings is the old Siegel-Cooper Dry Goods Store at 616–632 Sixth Ave. between 18th and 19th streets. It is a magnificent 1895 merchandising palace elaborately decorated with glazed terra cotta and marble columns.

The 1902 Flatiron Building, which stands on 23rd Street overlooking Madison Square, is one of the city's earliest—and still most famous—skyscrapers. Originally called the Fuller Building, the building got its present name from its triangular shape that fits the pie wedge formed by the junction of Broadway and Fifth Avenue.

Above: Trinity Church
Right: Siegel-Cooper Dry Goods Store
Far right: Flatiron Building

ARCHITECTURE

Chrysler Building

When it was built in 1930 the Chrysler Building was the tallest building in the world at 1,048 feet, but it held the record for only a few months before the Empire State Building shot past it.

What it lacks in height the Chrysler Building more than makes up in eccentric beauty. One of the first skyscrapers to use stainless steel over a large exposed surface, the Art Deco tower terminates in a scalloped, needlelike spire that is one of midtown Manhattan's most familiar landmarks. At night this spire's scores of triangular windows are outlined with brilliant fluorescent lighting, creating quite a show.

In homage to its original owner and patron stylized automotive motifs and designs appear throughout the building. Gargoyles resembling 1929 Chrysler radiator caps in the form of the winged god Mercury decorate the corners of the building's upper-floor setbacks. Inside, the triangular lobby is faced with African marble, and the doors of the paneled elevators are richly decorated.

The building was extensively renovated in 1981, and the lights in automotive style envisioned in architect William Van Allen's original plan were added at that time.

U.S. Custom House

At the tip of Lower Manhattan facing the small oval park called Bowling Green stands the monumental U.S. Custom House. An awesome granite palace built in 1907, it has been called by the American Institute of Architects "the *grandest* Beaux-Arts building in New York."

Now vacant, this seven-story landmark once held the offices of the Collector of Customs of the Port of New York (which moved to the nearby World Trade Center in the early '70s). Designed by Cass Gilbert, who also did the George Washington Bridge and the Woolworth Building, the Custom House is a museum in itself. The facade is graced with four enormous limestone sculptures by Daniel Chester French; they represent, in heroic female form, Africa, North America, Asia and Europe. Inside, around the ceiling of the spacious oval pavilion room, are 1930s murals by Reginald Marsh.

The site of the old U.S. Custom House is laden with history. Other structures that once stood here include the 17th-century Fort Amsterdam, the 18th-century Government House and a row of 19th-century townhouses. According to legend Bowling Green, the Custom House's front lawn, is the place where Peter Minuit "bought" Manhattan from the Manhattoes Indians for about $24 worth of cloth and trinkets.

Woolworth Building

The 1913 Woolworth Building—at 233 Broadway, across from City Hall—was for 17 years the tallest building in the world. Sixty stories tall from basement to tower, it is such a Gothic masterpiece that it has been called "The Cathedral of Commerce."

The three-story-high lobby and entranceway are marvels of a bygone era. The walls are faced with golden, veined Grecian marble. The vaulted ceiling is set with brilliantly colored glass mosaics, and the lacy wrought-iron cornices are covered in gold leaf. Note the large frescoes of "Commerce" and "Labor" and look for carved bas-relief caricatures of architect Cass Gilbert, builder Louis Horowitz and owner Frank W. Woolworth. At night the tower is brilliantly illuminated in white and green.

It is said that when Mr. Woolworth ordered the building as a headquarters for his five-and-10 empire, he paid for it in cash—a practice that would undoubtedly horrify modern tycoons.

Brooklyn Bridge

So important—and so beloved—is the Brooklyn Bridge that on its 100th birthday in 1983 the big celebration made headlines around the world. So inspirational is the bridge that it has been the subject of countless paintings, photos, poems, plays and motion pictures.

A man-made wonder in both design and engineering, the graceful bridge soars over the East River, connecting Manhattan at the City Hall area with Brooklyn at the base of Brooklyn Heights. Two enormous Gothic towers of granite blocks rise almost 300 feet above the water. They support

the cables, the steel suspenders and the 5,000 galvanized steel wires from which the 6,000-foot roadway platform is hung. The Brooklyn Bridge was the first bridge to connect New York with what later became its boroughs; it is still the most beautiful. You can drive across it, but the best way to experience its magnificence and to enjoy the spectacular views from the walkways and observation points is to walk it. Looking through the thousands of wires and cables is like looking through giant harps, which indeed they are when the wind whistles through them.

Washington Arch

Standing at the foot of Fifth Avenue, Washington Arch is the classical gateway to Washington Square in Greenwich Village. It commemorates the centennial of George Washington's first inauguration in 1789. First fashioned in wood by noted architect Stanford White in 1876, the arch proved so popular that funds were raised to re-create it in white marble for its dedication on May 4, 1895.

On either side of the monument's north facade, guarding the arch's pillars, is a statue of the nation's first president. The figure on the east side, showing Washington in uniform, was designed by Herman MacNeil; the one on the west, showing Washington in civilian clothes, is the work of A. Stirling Calder, father of the sculptor who created the now-classic mobiles.

The location in the heart of the Village has made Washington Arch and Washington Square favorite meeting places for generations of lovers, musicians, poets, political activists, sidewalk entertainers, chess and checkers players and students (the park serves as the campus for New York University). Some years ago a young man—probably the victim of a housing shortage—managed to enter a locked door on the arch's west pillar, climb to the large storage room at the top of the arch, and set up housekeeping there. He might have remained there for some time, but he attracted attention by hanging out his laundry on top of the monument.

St. Patrick's Cathedral

When St. Patrick's was built in 1879 upper Fifth Avenue was developing into a neighborhood of the rich and famous, as the city and its elite moved steadily northward. Townhouses and mansions interspersed with churches would characterize the avenue until commercialism, in the form of stores and hotels, would slowly take over after the turn of the century.

James Renwick, Jr., the architect of St. Patrick's, was already famous for another Gothic masterpiece, Grace Church at Broadway and 10th Street in Greenwich Village. If his St. Patrick's has never been as popular with architectural critics as Grace or other churches, the cathedral is nevertheless enormously popular with both residents and their guests. The main reviewing stand for the annual St. Patrick's Day Parade is placed on the cathedral's front steps, socially prominent weddings and funerals occur here in a steady stream, and in these activist days St. Patrick's is frequently the scene of one demonstration or another.

The English/French Gothic spires and granite walls of St. Patrick's were thoroughly cleaned for the cathedral's 100th birthday in 1979, revealing a more cheerful, less forbidding-looking structure. Of particular interest inside is the delicate Lady Chapel behind the high altar and the burial crypt where past cardinals are entombed.

Greene Street

SoHo Cast-Iron District

An area of 25 to 30 blocks just below Greenwich Village contains the finest collection of cast-iron buildings in the nation. SoHo, which stands for south of Houston Street (New Yorkers pronounce it "how-stun"), is bounded by Houston Street on the north, Canal Street on the south, Broadway on the east and Sixth Avenue on the west. This area dating from the 19th century was once threatened with demolition—city fathers wanted to run an expressway through the heart of it. Artists and preservationists turned it into an art colony in the 1960s. In 1973 the SoHo Cast-Iron Historic District was declared an official New York City landmark. Today SoHo is a prosperous neighborhood and a leading attraction for visitors.

The stunning cast-iron facades you see today—which were selected from catalogues and were, therefore, the first prefab buildings—were erected in the post–Civil War period as business headquarters, light manufacturing factories, textile companies and warehouses. Distinctive buildings to look for include the Haughwout Building at 488–492 Broadway (called by cast-iron historian and preservationist Margot Gayle "the most celebrated" building in the city), the 1871 Gunther Building at 469–475 Broome St. (once a fur dealer's headquarters, noted for its elegant, curved corner) and practically any building on Greene Street (an especially rich collection of neoclassical facades).

Villard Houses

From the outside the Villard Houses look like a single U-shaped Italian Renaissance palazzo, but they are actually four townhouses joined together. They were built in the late 1880s along Madison Avenue between 50th and 51st streets. Designed as lavish residences, they ended up in the first part of the 20th century as offices for Random House publishers and for the Roman Catholic Archdiocese of New York.

When these elegant but impractical houses were threatened with demolition hotel developer Harry Helmsley was persuaded to preserve the Villard group intact as the entranceway and public rooms for a hotel tower that would rise behind and above them. The result was the Helmsley Palace Hotel, which can rightly boast one of the most spectacular, most valuable lobby areas in the hospitality industry.

Whether or not you stay at the hotel—or have lunch, dinner or tea there—wander through the various public rooms to admire the rich paneling, the elaborately carved marble fireplaces, the coffered ceilings, the Tiffany glass and the La Farge murals.

Central Park

Manhattan's backyard, Central Park is a vast (843 acres—bigger than Monaco!) green carpet spread smack in the middle of an urban landscape.

Stretching from Central Park South to 125th Street, from Fifth Avenue to Central Park West, this fabulous greensward draws residents from all five boroughs of the city and visitors from around the world. They come here to stroll, bicycle, roller skate, ice skate, ride horseback, pitch horseshoes, play croquet and tennis, air their pets and children, fly kites, bat baseballs, toss footballs, sunbathe, picnic, attend free theater, listen to free music and opera, smell the flowers, admire the statuary, ride the carousel and a host of other activities.

The park was the brilliant design of two landscape geniuses, Frederick Law Olmsted and Calvert Vaux. All of it is worth your careful inspection, but essential stops include the Bethesda Fountain area near 72nd Street, the new zoo near East 64th Street and the Conservatory Garden near East 105th Street.

Rockefeller Center

Rockefeller Center remains after 60 years the perfect model of urban design. Begun in 1931 with 14 buildings on 12 acres, the center has grown into a 19-building complex covering 24 acres, with plans for future expansion.

More than just an architectural prototype whose lessons have been copied around the world, Rockefeller Center stands as a tribute to the Rockefeller family's idealism and faith in the future of a city. The buildings rose during the depth of the Great Depression—defying the rules of real estate development, giving employment to thousands, and reaffirming the ability of the American people to prevail and endure. Although detractors of the times called it "Rockefeller's Folly," critics of today label the center architecturally excellent, an outstanding urban complex.

Taking the bows was a team of architectural firms, but the names most remembered are Wallace Harrison and Raymond Hood.

The GE Building (formerly the RCA Building) at 30 Rockefeller Plaza is the center's soaring, 70-story centerpiece. A sleek and slender slab of limestone and steel, it faces the center's sunken plaza with its gold-plated statue of Prometheus, who presides over a splashing fountain in summer and a public skating rink in winter. Stretching from the Lower Plaza to Fifth Avenue are the fountains and flowers of the Channel Gardens, so named because they lie between the low (seven stories) French and English buildings, which front on the avenue between 49th and 50th streets.

Grand Central Terminal

One of the world's most famous, most frequented hubs, Grand Central Station—as New Yorkers call it—is a synonym for human congestion. It contains the city's largest and busiest public room—275 feet long, 120 feet wide and 125 feet high. It is also known as one of the world's greatest railway passenger terminals. Here, hundreds of thousands of commuters daily use the suburban routes and the three subway systems that interconnect underground to serve the entire city.

An architectural wonder since it was built, between 1903 and 1913, the classic Beaux-Arts building stands on East 42nd Street facing down Park Avenue. Surmounting the facade is a gigantic clock and group sculpture arrangement called "Transportation," which features the central figure of Mercury, the god of speed, flanked by Minerva, the goddess of strength and wisdom, and Hercules, who symbolizes physical strength and energy. The limestone group weighs more than 1,000 tons and stands 48 feet high. It was designed by Warren and Wetmore and sculpted by Jules-Felix Coutan. Below this group, framed in the station's huge central window, is a heroic bronze statue of railroad and steamship magnate Cornelius Vanderbilt.

Grand Central recently underwent a multimillion-dollar restoration and renovation, and to see it at its best—while picking up a detailed history—take one of the regularly scheduled free tours.

Cathedral of St. John the Divine

St. John the Divine—the Byzantine-Romanesque-French Gothic structure firmly planted on Amsterdam Avenue at 112th Street in Morningside Heights—is the largest cathedral in the world. (St. Peter's in Rome is a church, not a cathedral.)

Begun in 1892 (and still building), St. John's is 601 feet long and 320 feet wide. It's so huge that if you're going to a wedding or funeral in a back chapel, you should arrive at least 30 minutes ahead of time in order to make your way through the cathedral. Originally designed by the firm of Heins and La Farge and later by Cram and Ferguson, the cathedral is, like all enormous religious structures built over many years, a result of many hands. From the outside, you can tell the structure is still unfinished—the facade's twin towers are yet to be built. Inside, all seems in complete working order. Of special interest are the side aisles, which rise to the same height as the great nave, the baptistery and the chapels around the apse.

St. John the Divine is a good citizen as well as a great cathedral, serving its ethnically mixed neighborhood with outreach programs, special music and theater events, art shows, lectures and interfaith ceremonies. Next to the cathedral is an operating stone masonry shed, where dozens of artisans, many of them area youths, are learning to carve as it was done centuries ago.

Belmont Racetrack

Aqueduct and Belmont Racetracks

Aqueduct is one of two facilities right within the confines of New York City where you can enjoy the Sport of Kings. Thoroughbred flat races are held six days a week during the season, which runs from mid-October to early May.

Aqueduct, which is located in Ozone Park, Queens, can accommodate up to 90,000 attendees. It's the only racing track that has its own subway station. You can take the A train (yes, there really is such a train) directly to the Aqueduct Racetrack stop.

The original Aqueduct Racetrack opened in 1894 and has been rebuilt and extensively renovated on several occasions, including a major facelift carried out in the late 1980s. Aqueduct has several dining facilities, the most elegant of which is the Aqueduct Skyline Club's Equestris Dining Room.

Belmont Racetrack in Elmont, Long Island, has about the same attendance capacity as Aqueduct. Opened in 1905, Belmont's season runs from early May to late July and picks up again from late August to early October. In between, the New York Racing Association's summer thoroughbred racing season takes place at Saratoga, in upstate New York. As at Aqueduct races are scheduled at Belmont six days a week during the season. The biggest annual event is the Belmont Stakes, which takes place in June and pits top three-year-olds against each other. It's the last leg of the prestigious Triple Crown, which carries a $500,000 purse.

The best way to get to see "Beautiful Belmont," as its fans call it, is on a delightful Breakfast at Belmont tour, offered on Saturdays, Sundays and holidays from 7 a.m. to 9:30 a.m. It includes a paddock show, a gate demonstration and a tour of the backstretch area on a tram.

Belmont has several restaurants, including the Paddock Dining Room, a cafeteria and the Garden Terrace, where you can enjoy clubhouse lunches with closed-circuit TV. Jockeys will answer your questions while you eat.

Yankee Stadium

The home of the Bronx Bombers was built in 1923 at River Avenue and East 161st Street in the Bronx, and it was almost immediately nicknamed "The House that Ruth Built" in honor of the most famous Yankee of them all, Babe Ruth. In addition to Ruth, Lou Gehrig, Joltin' Joe DiMaggio, Casey Stengel and Mickey Mantle are among the celebrated New York Yankees who have been honored with special monuments in the park. These monuments used to be in center field, where the players frequently had to go behind them to retrieve a long hit. After the renovation in the 1970s, the monuments were moved to Monument Park between the bullpens.

The entire stadium complex is 11.6 acres, with the field itself occupying 3.5 acres. It normally has 57,545 seats, but it can be configured to seat more. In 1976 the city carried out a reconstruction of Yankee Stadium on the same site, which cost about $100 million (almost 50 times the price tag for the original stadium). The project improved viewing, modernized facilities and expanded the amount of parking space available.

For about 15 years the New York Giants played here, and throughout Yankee Stadium's history major boxing matches have also taken place here, including the much-publicized grudge match in June of 1938 when Joe Louis decked Max Schmeling in the first round.

People have also thronged the stadium to hear Popes Paul VI and John Paul II celebrate mass and to hear other religious leaders address their flocks. For a time Yankee Stadium reigned as the venue of choice for cult leaders who claimed to have the inside scoop on when the end of the world was scheduled to take place and invited their followers to join them at the stadium for the big event. Their credibility was sorely tried when the day after each announced doomsday the cry, "Play ball!" once again was heard in Yankee Stadium.

Monument Park

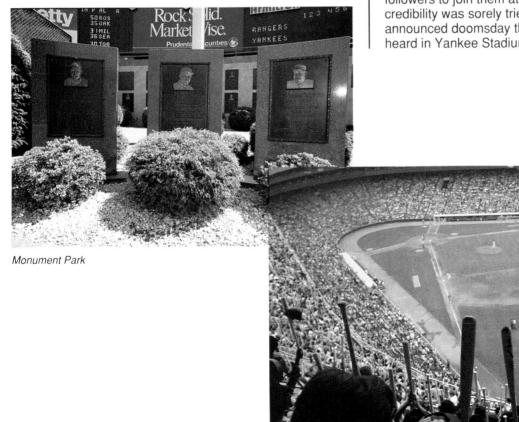

There's so much to see and do at the Flushing Meadows–Corona Park Complex besides events at Shea Stadium that it's worth coming a little early or staying after the ball game so you can be sure to catch some of the other sights. Some of them are the Ice Skating Rink and the Hall of Science, both built for the 1964–65 World's Fair; the Queens Museum, which contains the 15,000-square-foot model of New York City featured in the World's Fair; the Queens Children's Zoo; Theatre-in-the-Park and Playground for All Children; and the U.S. Tennis Association National Tennis Center.

Shea Stadium

The New York Mets have succeeded the Brooklyn Dodgers in the hearts of New Yorkers as the city's favorite underdog baseball team. In 1964 a home was built for the Amazin' Mets in Flushing Meadows, Queens. Construction coincided with the 1964–65 New York World's Fair, which occupied a site adjacent to Shea Stadium at Flushing Meadows–Corona Park. The stadium was erected during the administration of New York City's famous master builder, Parks Commissioner Robert Moses, and was named for a city official, Planning Commission Chief of Staff Col. William J. Shea.

Though not as monumental or architecturally noteworthy as Yankee Stadium, Shea Stadium has been singled out for its excellent sight lines and high-tech features, including its powerful Diamond-vision video screen. Shea Stadium was designed with rotating seating tiers so it could accommodate 55,000 people for baseball games and in football season 60,000 people for New York Jets games. However, several seasons ago the Jets, despite their designation as a New York team, packed up their jerseys and moved across the Hudson River to the Meadowlands Sports Complex in New Jersey. All that space doesn't go to waste, however, when the Mets aren't around. Like Yankee Stadium and Madison Square Garden, Shea also hosts entertainment presentations and special events programs.

Madison Square Garden

Though it's no longer located at Madison Square, New York's premier sports and entertainment venue is still known by the same name as the original stadium. Built during the latter part of the last century at Madison Avenue and 26th Street, the first Madison Square Garden was a roofless building with walls almost 30 feet wide. It was erected on the site where P.T. Barnum's famous Hippodrome had stood, and it was constructed to house concerts, shows and exhibitions. A fire destroyed the first Garden in 1889, but it was soon replaced by another at the same location. This second version was designed by famous architect and bon vivant Stanford White. And it was at the Garden in 1906 that White, who was attending a party, was shot and killed by Harry K. Thaw, the millionaire husband of chorus girl Evelyn Nesbit, who had been White's young paramour.

By the time the third version opened on Eighth Avenue between 49th and 50th streets, Madison Square Garden had become synonymous with major sports events. The fourth and present Garden, which opened in 1968, is situated on the site of the former Pennsylvania Station, from Seventh to Eighth avenues between 31st and 33rd streets. The New York Knicks basketball team and the New York Rangers hockey team both call Madison Square Garden home.

The Garden is in the process of expanding its principal venues, which include the 4,700-seat Felt Forum and the 20,500-seat Arena. Surrounding the Arena is a 50,000-square-foot exhibition area where large trade shows and other special events are held. A 48-lane bowling center here is frequented by professional bowlers.

In total, this enormous complex hosts more than 600 events every year, which are attended by approximately 6 million people. A mind-boggling array of sporting events, entertainment shows and special events take place at the Garden, including the Ringling Bros. and Barnum & Bailey Circus, Ice Capades, International Cat Show, Westminster Kennel Club Dog Show and National Horse Show. The Garden hosts championship boxing matches, tennis, gymnastic competitions, track and field races, rodeos, drama and dance productions, rock and country-and-western concerts, and even some presidential conventions, including the 1976 and 1980 Democratic National Conventions.

Meadowlands Sports Complex

The Meadowlands opened in 1976 in East Rutherford, N.J., just across the Hudson from New York City. The complex consists of three main facilities on a 750-acre site and was built at a cost of $450 million.

Giants Stadium, home of the New York Jets and the New York Giants, has a seating capacity of 76,891. The stadium is a mecca for football fans. It launches the college football season every fall with the Kickoff Classic, a preseason bowl game that spotlights two or three top teams from the previous year, and hosts NCAA football games. The stadium is fitted out with state-of-the-art facilities including two computerized video-matrix boards that flash the latest scores and give fans a second look at the action via instant replay. When it's not football season the stadium is used for concerts and other entertainment programs.

The Brendan Byrne Arena is a sports and entertainment venue that was inaugurated in 1981 by New Jersey's own Bruce Springsteen at six sold-out concert performances. It seats approximately 21,000 depending on the event. The National Hockey League, the New Jersey Devils, the National Basketball Association and the New Jersey Nets have all played in the arena. The arena also hosts boxing and wrestling matches, track and field events and college basketball games.

In addition, the arena is the setting for concerts, family entertainment programs, the Ringling Bros. and Barnum & Bailey Circus and the Ice Capades.

The Meadowlands Racetrack, which can accommodate 40,000 people, offers year-round night racing. Its schedule includes harness racing from January to August and thoroughbred racing from September through December. Important harness-racing events scheduled include the Hambletonian Stakes, the $1 million Meadowlands Pace and the $1.5 million Woodrow Wilson Pace. For fans of thoroughbred racing there's the $500,000 Young America race and the Meadowlands Cup.

U.S. Tennis Association (USTA) National Tennis Center

Like Shea Stadium, the USTA National Tennis Center is located in the 1,255-acre Flushing Meadows–Corona Park, New York's second largest park. It was built as a performance hall for the 1964–65 World's Fair.

The U.S. Open is one of the world's most prestigious tennis tournaments, with top prize money running more than $300,000. It had previously been held at Forest Hills, N.Y. In the late 1970s, when tennis became America's fastest-growing sport, organizers of the U.S. Open started looking around for new, bigger quarters. In the summer of 1978 the U.S. Open moved to Flushing Meadows.

The USTA National Tennis Center has 27 lighted outdoor courts and nine indoor courts and is still growing. With interest in tennis still running high—more than 447,000 people attended the 1990 U.S. Open—the center recently announced plans to launch a major expansion of its facilities.

Some of tennis's most dramatic moments have taken place at Flushing Meadows. In 1979 after Bjorn Borg defeated Roscoe Tanner at Wimbledon in a dramatic five-set match, the two adversaries met in New York, and this time Tanner's 140-mile-per-hour serve broke the net, giving him a four-set victory (although in the end McEnroe won, defeating Gerulaitis). Two years later in 1981 John McEnroe became the first man since 1925 to win the singles more than two years in a row.

In 1986 the U.S. Open celebrated the 100th anniversary of Women's Championships with a special ceremony, and in 1988 one of the great women players of all time, Steffi Graf, won her first U.S. Open singles title and completed the first women's grand slam since Margaret Smith Court's in 1970. It was also the first grand slam ever at Flushing Meadows (the previous five had all taken place at Forest Hills).

The Rainbow Room

Midtown Nightlife

The most dazzling, romantic night spots in the city are found in midtown Manhattan in and around the major hotels. The clubs and cabarets located in the hotels themselves have the advantage of being on the hotel guests' doorstep. Charges can be put on the hotel bill—registered guests often get special rates and privileges—and there's no trouble or expense in getting to or from the club.

Long-established favorites in this category are the lovely, wood-paneled Oak Room in the Algonquin Hotel and the stylish, intimate Cafe Carlyle in the fashionable Hotel Carlyle. The Oak Room has presented such cabaret legends as Julie Wilson, Karen Akers, Steve Ross, Margaret Whiting and Michael Feinstein; at the Cafe Carlyle, such stars as Eartha Kitt and Dixie Carter croon to the fans.

The next category of midtown night spots is the big-time, big-deal nightclub, often with spectacular decor and an international reputation. The most famous of these clubs is the glorious Art Deco masterpiece the Rainbow Room, located on the 65th floor of Rockefeller Center's GE Building. The Rainbow Room, which has recently been restored to its 1930s glory, is the archetype of all the penthouse nightclubs seen in the Rogers and Astaire movies. Wide staircases allow patrons to make a grand entrance, tables with custom-designed appointments are arranged on several levels, and a huge crystal chandelier casts a glow on the revolving circular dance floor where a cosmopolitan crowd dances to a top band. Competing with all this grandeur is one of the most famous wraparound views of New York's skyline.

Midtown Manhattan is also the home of the old-fashioned nightclub, usually on the ground floor of an apartment house or brownstone. It has a bar up front where singles can often get a view of the show in the back room. Leading lights in this category include Michael's Pub at 211 E. 55th St., where performances range from groups like the George Shearing Quartet to concert versions of classic musicals, and Don't Tell Mama at 343 W. 46th St., which specializes in solo singers, comedians and mini-musical revues.

Comedy Clubs

Thanks largely to the rising popularity of the stand-up comedy star on TV, comedy clubs have proliferated in New York in recent years. The leading Manhattan comedy clubs are in midtown, on the Upper East Side and the Upper West Side, in Chelsea and in Greenwich Village. Both Catch a Rising Star and The Comic Strip are open seven days a week and are great Upper East Side spots for discovering budding talent—stand-up comics and singers. Dangerfield's, also in that area, is owned by Rodney Dangerfield, and he books comics you can respect. In the Village, MacDougal Street below Washington Square is reliable comedy-club territory. On Bleecker Street is Art D'Lugoff's venerable Village Gate, a huge barn of a place that contains several theaters where comics, comedy revues and comedy groups are frequently presented. The Duplex, in its handsome new quarters at Sheridan Square and Christopher Street, showcases award-winning comedy/improv acts.

Most of the performers you see in these clubs will be fledgling comics. Once they catch on or make it to the big time, they move to larger venues.

Jazz Clubs

Jazz is enjoying a renaissance in the Big Apple. Although jazz clubs are located all over Manhattan—the Upper West Side, Upper East Side and of course Harlem—the greatest concentration these days is in Greenwich Village. In the Village's basements, bars, storefronts and restaurants are the hottest clubs in town. The Village Vanguard is a simple basement room down a steep flight of steps, but it offers some of the hottest jazz being played today—from the Branford Marsalis Trio to the 17-piece Mel Lewis Big Band. Sweet Basil, a brick-walled bar/restaurant with an enclosed sidewalk cafe area, presents three shows nightly from 10 o'clock. Bradley's, which is everybody's favorite jazz bar, is the place for relaxing and unwinding to stellar performers like pianist Billy Mays and bassist Ray Drummond. Just above the Village on the East Side is the restaurant and jazz club Condon's, where singers like Chris Conner and Jimmy Witherspoon do their gigs; and another basement room that heats up nightly with such groups as the Charlie Byrd Trio and the Les Paul Trio is Fat Tuesday's.

Jazz plays throughout the year in New York, but the scene really heats up during George Wein's annual JVC Jazz Festival during the last week in June and the first week in July.

The Limelight

Dance Clubs

Because the dance club scene is a volatile one, an enduring favorite is a rare nightbird. The Limelight is an '80s club that's as hot as ever—particularly on Wednesday night when Disco 2000 is the theme. Most clubs seem to come and go with the seasons. How to find what's "in" or "out"? There's no scientifically exact way, but here are a few pointers. Read the columns and the ads in publications that keep up with the scene: the Village Voice, New York magazine, the New Yorker and the daily papers. Go to one club and listen to word of mouth about other clubs. Remember that the trend is definitely toward downtown clubs—in Chelsea, Greenwich Village, SoHo, TriBeCa (a neighborhood near SoHo) and Lower Manhattan.

As for what to wear to the clubs, there are generally three ways to go: young, chic, with-it fashions—what locals call "New York dressy"; weird or outrageous styles that will make you stand out in a crowd; or—a style that often works very well, especially with the older crowd—black-tie formal. Although none of the clubs has a strict dress code, you do have to pass muster with the guards at the door, who are firmly told not to admit trouble-makers or anyone who won't add to the glamour and excitement of the club. So it does pay to look as young and beautiful or as distinguished and presentable as possible.

Once inside you are free to roam the establishment. In addition to a large area for dancing—and you can take to the floor solo as well as with a partner—clubs usually have areas for overlooking the action and bar lounges for relaxing. Some club visitors never dance but come just to make the scene.

Cabaret

Cabaret in New York is usually one performer—a singer or a singer/pianist—whose evening repertoire is built around a theme: "An Evening of Cole Porter," for example, or "A Salute to Stephen Sondheim." The usual material is classic standards, Broadway show tunes and hit songs from Hollywood musicals.

Certain cabarets specialize in one-of-a-kind performers and groups. For example, The Ballroom, in Chelsea, regularly presents La Gran Scena Opera Company, an all-male group performing arias from the standard opera repertory; magic artist Jeff McBride, whose act is a wondrous blend of magic, mime, Kabuki, dance and new-wave music; and the wild and wacky singer/pianist/stand-up comic Phoebe Legere. In Greenwich Village at the new, ultramodern duplex club called Eighty Eights, visitors to the comfortable upstairs cabaret room can hear group and solo performers that are bright new downtown acts on the road to uptown fame.

The most notable new spots, destined to become classics, are Rainbow & Stars, a jewel box of a cabaret next to the Rainbow Room, and the Cabaret at the Russian Tea Room, upstairs at the famous celebrity restaurant next to Carnegie Hall.

Cabarets often have two shows a night, especially on weekends—an early dinner show and an after-theater supper show. Many patrons come just for drinks and the performance, paying a cover charge and a minimum.

Rainbow & Stars

Zinno

The Lone Star Cafe

Piano Rooms

The "cocktail piano" hour has been a New York tradition in midtown bars and hotel lounges since the 1920s and '30s; supplementing this pleasant ritual is the recent trend of offering cocktail and jazz pianists in fine restaurants throughout the city, especially upscale Italian spots, in an effort to attract customers. Zinno in Greenwich Village is a sleek, cozy bar and restaurant on the ground floor of an old townhouse. In midtown the Assembly—a steak and seafood house at 16 W. 51st St.—offers a pianists in the lounge each weekday evening. Bruno, La Camelia and Sign of the Dove on the Upper East Side all offer pianists or pianist/singers to accompany a meal.

Piano bars, where customers are encouraged to join in the fun, are for the most part concentrated in Greenwich Village. In fact Grove Street, leading west off Seventh Avenue at Sheridan Square, can be called the heart of Manhattan's red-hot piano-bar district. In this one street your ears will lead you to such well-known watering holes as Arthur's Tavern and the Five Oaks, which throb with passionate enthusiasm until the wee hours.

Pop/Rock

The pop/rock scene—to which rap is now added—is such a popular one these days that any appearance or concert by top stars must be booked into one of the city's huge halls. Such luminaries as Frank Sinatra, Liza Minnelli, the Grateful Dead, Diana Ross or Sting always head for such monster venues as Madison Square Garden (20,000 seats), Radio City Music Hall (6,000 seats) and Carnegie Hall (almost 3,000 seats)—and even then their tickets sell out soon after they're put on sale.

Some pop stars play Broadway theaters for extended runs. Judy Garland was a smash hit in her Palace Theatre engagements, and recent pop artists who have taken to the stage for sold-out runs include Michael Feinstein and Harry Connick, Jr.

Other top pop/rock stars prefer to meet their fans in a more intimate setting. Peggy Lee regularly checks into The Ballroom (see "Cabaret") for several weeks at a time. The Bottom Line, in Greenwich Village, attracts such names as Kris Kristofferson, Chico Hamilton and Buster Poindexter. Other well-known clubs are the Ritz, for rock acts of national caliber; S.O.B.'s, for reggae; the Lone Star Cafe, for blues, country and American roots music; and CBGB's, where the United States "punk" scene began.

Midtown

The glitz and glamour of midtown merchandising has helped New York win the title as "Shopping Capital of the World." Any visitor is likely to fall under the spell of Manhattan's famous midtown department stores. Their window displays are works of art and help to establish trends around the world. Inside, on floor after floor, the presentation of merchandise is enticing and exciting; and the black-tie parties to open a new department or launch a new promotion are celebrity events that make all the society columns. Most important of all, the big-time department stores have *everything;* they are the ultimate in one-stop shopping.

Although some department stores might specialize in a particular line of merchandise (high fashions for women, home furnishings, gift items), most are full-service emporiums. Almost all of the stores locate their cosmetics department on the first floor (where you can get free makeup advice and a free spritz of perfume), with other departments easily reached by elevator or escalator: gourmet foods, housewares, bedding, rugs and furniture, children's wear and everything else you might want.

New York not only boasts the world's largest department store—Macy's, which covers an entire city block—but also the famous and influential Bloomingdale's. A decade or so ago it was predicted that the rise of suburban malls would sound the death knell of the inner-city department store. That prophecy fell flat; customers discovered that nothing beats the thrill of the urban shopping experience.

The department stores of Midtown Manhattan are concentrated in three separate but nearby areas: Fifth Avenue, the Upper East Side along Lexington and Third avenues in the 50s, and in Herald Square where Broadway meets 34th street.

F.A.O. Schwarz

Who can forget the scene in the movie "Big," when Tom Hanks, playing a young boy living inside a man's body, dances on the huge piano keyboard, punching out "Heart and Soul"? The scene took place in the world's most famous toy store, F.A.O. Schwarz, a vast wonderland in the General Motors Building at Fifth Avenue between 58th and 59th streets.

Parents don't resist taking their children here—they want to come so much themselves. It's like walking into a fairy-tale world made of gingerbread houses and Peter Pan landscapes, or a universe of high-tech gadgets and games.

If a child—or child at heart—wants it, this magnificent store can provide it. It has giant stuffed animals (giraffes, elephants and jungle cats), walk-in doll houses, rocking horses, electric trains, dolls (from plain, hand-crafted, one-of-a-kind rag dolls to fancy, haute-couture debutantes and princesses), teddy bears in all sizes and, of course, toy cars, trucks, trains, boats and planes. For the thoroughly up-to-date child, there is a whole department of video games, computers and mechanical toys (including robots). Be prepared to spend at least an hour or two just browsing this magical kingdom.

Madison Avenue

In the one mile along Madison Avenue, from 59th to 79th streets, stand some of the finest and most exclusive shops and art galleries in New York. In elegance, style and quality, the avenue's wares have been compared to those found on London's Bond Street or Rome's Via Condotti.

Late morning or early afternoon during the week is the time to "do" Madison Avenue—the crowds are light, the customers classy. But if you also like to people-watch as well as window-shop, go before and after brunch on Saturday.

Clothing boutiques representing the leading designers in Paris, Rome and London offer the latest styles in women's and men's fashions. The Italian and Spanish leather emporiums, which smell as rich as they look, will outfit you with everything from handbags and luggage to boots and saddles. Silver and china, fabrics and needlework, exquisite linens, shoes and sweaters, antique and modern jewelry, clocks and watches, books, posters, cosmetics and gourmet foods—all of these are just a few of the treasures awaiting your inspection.

Art galleries representing works by classic and modern painters and sculptors are dotted throughout the avenue and on the side streets leading from it. Individual and group shows change frequently and are listed and described in such publications as The New Yorker and New York magazine.

F.A.O. Schwarz

Fifth Avenue

Fifth Avenue, which begins at Washington Square in Greenwich Village and ends at the Harlem River in Upper Manhattan, runs through neighborhoods both residential and commercial. By far the most famous stretch is the one-mile Fifth Avenue shopping district between 39th and 59th streets.

Within this "Golden Mile" lie some of the world's most respected names in women's and men's fashions, jewelry, crystal, china and home furnishings—Tiffany & Company, Bergdorf Goodman and many others. Several of the world's leading booksellers, including Barnes & Noble, are represented here, as is F.A.O. Schwarz, the renowned toy store. There is a celebrated house of beauty, a venerable London tobacconist and two boutiques dispensing the finest in imported chocolates. There are shops serving as outlets for the ultimate in Italian leatherwear and luggage. Even the Metropolitan Museum of Art has come down the avenue to the shopping district; its large new gift shop is located in Rockefeller Center's Channel Gardens.

Walking and window shopping—this is the only way to "do" the Fifth Avenue stores. Perhaps the best starting point for a stroll is the Grand Army Plaza at the southeast corner of Central Park and 59th Street, just opposite the Plaza Hotel. The most elegant shops and stores are located in the 50s, and it is here that you will see the most fashionably dressed New Yorkers, especially in the late morning or early afternoon.

On your first foray down the avenue it would probably be best to stick to window shopping, making mental notes of the places you later wish to shop. Lucky you if you're in town between Thanksgiving and New Year's. Fifth Avenue's holiday window displays are not only works of art but theater for the whole family. Most are elaborately animated, and some have a theme, such as "An Old-Fashioned Christmas in Victorian Times."

Even though the Fifth Avenue stores are among the most exclusive you will find anywhere, they are not above having sales—and splendid ones at that. Such fashion-conscious establishments want to get rid of merchandise fast to make room for what's new.

Antiques and Collectibles

Whether you're looking for Empire clocks, 1920s radios, early baseball cards, Georgian furniture or 19th century music boxes, you are strongly advised to stroll through two fabulous midtown centers: Place des Antiquaires, 125 E. 57th St., and Manhattan Arts & Antiques Center, 1050 Second Ave. at 55th Street. Not only will you see scores of dealers—and thousands of different items in one spot—you can pick up a wealth of valuable information on where to continue your shopping expeditions. The Upper East Side auction houses—Christie's at 502 Park Ave. at 59th Street, Christie's East at 219 E. 67th St., and Sotheby's at 411 E. 76th St. and at 1334 York Ave.—are great magnets for the antiques and collectibles customer, as are the regularly scheduled antique shows.

Once you have been briefed on the general scene try several areas for exploring. West 45th Street just off Fifth Avenue is good for antique silver and old silver patterns. The flea markets at Columbus and 76th Street (Sundays), Sixth Avenue at 26th Street (weekends) and Greenwich Village on the side streets west of Seventh Avenue (especially Bleecker, Christopher and Hudson) can be productive hunting areas. Lower Broadway between 14th and 9th streets is good for antique furniture, paintings and decorative items.

Upper East Side

As you'd expect in Manhattan's most sophisticated, most dignified, most expensive neighborhood, the Upper East Side shops are top of the line in both quality and price.

Mainly a residential neighborhood, the Upper East Side consists of townhouses and apartment buildings along the side streets from the 50s through the 80s, with stores and other commercial enterprises along the avenues. Except for Alexander's and Bloomingdale's on Lexington and Third avenues in the 50s—plus the art galleries, gift shops and clothing outlets along Madison Avenue—the shops are small, serving the neighborhood's need for food, flowers, casual clothing, housewares, sporting goods, cards and stationery.

At one time—back in the 1940s and '50s, before the elevated train structure came down—Third Avenue on the Upper East Side was lined with antique shops, located in the storefronts of brownstones and tenements. Now almost all of the low-rise buildings are gone, replaced with skyscraper apartment or commercial buildings. A few lovely shops remain, however, and the antiques and collectibles they offer (period furniture, china and crystal, clocks and music boxes, 19th-century landscape paintings and portraits) are superb.

One unusual and essential East Side shopping experience is the United Nations (entrance on First Avenue at 46th Street). The basement gift shops are an international bazaar offering thousands of quality items from member nations around the globe. There is also an international bookshop—you can pick up UNESCO greeting cards—and the incomparable United Nations Post Office.

Chick Darrow's Fun Antiques & Collectibles

Open-air flea market at Columbus and 76th

Zabar's

Columbus Avenue and Upper West Side

The Upper West Side is an old, established residential neighborhood into which young professionals and office workers have moved. Until their arrival beginning about 20 years ago shopping was mainly confined to the essential-services category. For serious shopping residents used to take the bus or subway down to Herald Square and the Lower East Side or over to Fifth Avenue and the Upper East Side. With the arrival of the Yuppies, neighborhood stores and shops moved in to service their needs. Today the main avenues running north out of the Lincoln Center area—Columbus, Amsterdam and Broadway—are lined with trendy clothing boutiques, video and CD outlets, ethnic food stores, gift shops and costume jewelry shops. The turnover is great—a store will completely change character overnight—because so much of the merchandise depends on fads, which can vanish in a flash.

The Sunday open-air flea market in the vacant lot at Columbus Avenue and 76th Street is a great place to people-watch as well as shop. The mixture is eclectic to say the least, and not all the items are genuinely old and funky. Nevertheless, the careful, patient shopper can find excellent gifts, and the antique jewelry is a particularly good buy. Columbus Avenue is also well known throughout the city for its fine—and reasonable—rug stores.

Amsterdam Avenue in the 70s is the place to look for small shops specializing in women's clothing. The area also has a reputation for small antiques, memorabilia and gift items.

Upper Broadway is the area to browse for gourmet foods and kitchenware. Zabar's, covering most of its block, draws customers and mail orders from around the world. Exotic coffees and cheeses, unusual jams and jellies, smoked meats and fish—all make much-appreciated gifts and take-home items.

Lincoln Center, in the 60s along Broadway, has a number of gift shops in its various buildings, and the Metropolitan Opera and Avery Fisher Hall shops are standouts. In addition to the expected T-shirts, recordings and libretti, you can find a host of fun items—all with a musical motif—such as umbrellas, shower curtains and greeting cards.

Gourmet Food Shops

Because many gourmet foods are sold unpackaged, unprocessed and highly perishable, the stores selling them are located all over town, serving their immediate neighborhoods. But certain shops are worth a trip from anywhere.

Greenwich Village and SoHo, areas of sophisticated tastes and sensitive palates, are laden with enticements for the gourmet. In the Village gourmet food shops can be found on Sixth Avenue above 8th Street and along Bleecker Street east of Seventh Avenue. Because of the neighborhood's strong Italian background—at one time Bleecker was lined with fruit and vegetable pushcarts— most of the stores specialize in Italian foods. You'll find Italian herbs and spices, virgin olive oils and aromatic vinegars, bread and baked goods, salamis and cheeses (especially mozzarella, gorgonzola and goat cheeses), pastas of all shapes and sizes and colors, and a wide variety of imported canned mushrooms and smoked fish. Some stores even concentrate on one type of food: stores selling fresh pasta made on the premises and pork stores selling all of the pig from ears to feet.

SoHo, along Prince and Spring streets and on its eastern boundary Broadway, has large and small gourmet food stores—again, many with an Italian or continental touch. Some places even have counters or cafes where you can sip espresso and sample an Italian pastry or a dish of gelato.

The Upper West Side in the 70s and 80s is another rich area for gourmet foods, as are the food departments of the big department stores.

The Diamond District

Even if you're not the least bit interested in gems and jewelry—or have no very special person on your gift list— you owe it to yourself to see 47th Street between Fifth and Sixth avenues.

It's an only-in-New-York experience. Bearded diamond dealers in full Hasidic attire—long black coats, big black hats, black suits and shoes—dash here and there with formidable black briefcases or satchels. Customers, messengers, delivery boys, carts and trucks crowd the street and sidewalks. Everyone seems in a hurry or a high state of excitement.

The large and small shops and stores that line both sides of the street have window displays jammed with jewels of all sizes in settings of all styles. The intense lighting focused on these gems creates a blazing—almost blinding—effect.

From a buyer's standpoint, it's a situation in which the buyer should beware. If you're looking to buy, educate yourself beforehand, comparison-shop, resist pressure and, if possible, bring along an expert. Checking the jewelry stores in your own home town or, after you arrive, stopping in one of the leading Fifth Avenue jewelers (where prices and quality are inflexible) would be wise preparatory moves.

R.J. King & Co. on Bleecker Street

Greenwich Village, the East Village and SoHo

For years Greenwich Village—or more properly the West Village that lies west of Fifth Avenue—has been a shopper's paradise. The shops and boutiques are small, the service friendly and helpful, and the merchandise is among the most imaginative in town—as you would expect in an area that has always attracted artists, actors, writers, intellectuals and students.

Walking is the best way to shop in this area. A good starting point is Sheridan Square and Seventh Avenue. From here walk west on Christopher Street to Hudson Street, turn right on Hudson and walk roughly north a few blocks to the point where it meets Bleecker Street, turn right on Bleecker and backtrack to complete a rough triangle. You'll run into antique shops, gift shops, boutiques displaying exotic objets d'art, leather-goods stores, imported-furniture outlets (Georgian desks, French Country dining sets), print and poster galleries, rare-book stores, wine stores, coffee and tea importers and an irresistible hand-made chocolates shop.

The East Village, which lies east of Broadway and is often called NoHo (for north of Houston Street) in some parts, is a much trendier, funkier, more laid-back and ethnically mixed area. St. Mark's Place, leading east out of Astor Place, was the heart of Hippieville in the 1960s and early '70s, and although the flower children are now long gone the East Village is still a relaxed and unconventional neighborhood. The avant-garde is the pervading philosophy of the book stores and art galleries you'll visit.

At times it will seem that the entire East Village is one sidewalk flea market. The areas around Cooper Union and Astor Place are filled with individual vendors selling their wares on wall-to-wall blankets and beach towels. Books, magazines, household items, radios, watches, men's and women's clothing, costume jewelry—most of it secondhand—are spread out in such profusion that navigating the streets becomes difficult to impossible.

SoHo (south of Houston Street) is as upscale as the East Village is bohemian. It became New York's downtown art colony back in the '60s, when artists moved into the spacious lofts vacated by small manufacturers, but it rapidly turned into an area of posh apartments, topflight art galleries, trendy clothing stores, gourmet food emporiums and celebrity restaurants. Virtually all of the SoHo galleries specialize in contemporary art—from the works of modern masters such as Andy Warhol, Jasper Johns and Robert Rauschenberg to the wildest and wackiest works by conceptual and environmental artists.

West Broadway from Houston to Canal streets is SoHo's main north-south drag, with Prince and Spring streets the principal cross streets. Many of the most important galleries and shops—and almost all of the restaurants—are located on these streets. But don't overlook the galleries and shops on the north-south streets: Wooster, Greene and Mercer. The art is just as startling, the clothing just as with-it, and the atmosphere is much more relaxed.

Outdoor shopping in the East Village

Discount Emporiums

To hear a New Yorker talk no true shopper would dream of buying anything except at a discount. Women head for the marked-down fashions at the shopping centers in the Bronx and Brooklyn, the upscale thrift shops on 57th Street, or the discount fashion and accessories shops on Seventh Avenue in the 20s. Men head for the discounted menswear stores on Broadway in the 20s, on upper Broadway in the 70s and 80s and in Lower Manhattan near City Hall. Everyone goes to the Lower East Side, and everyone looks for citywide sales, especially the ones following Christmas and New Year's and those marking such holidays as Presidents' Day in February, Memorial Day and July Fourth.

Electronic equipment, computers, cameras, copiers and fax machines can be bought at most attractive prices on West 45th Street between Sixth Avenue and Broadway, on Broadway in the 30s, or along Lexington and Madison avenues in the 40s. But buyer beware! Know what you want and about what it's worth. Read up and comparison-shop. Best of all, take a friend or relative with whom you can compare notes. The effort will be worth it: Experts insist that the prices are lower than Hong Kong's.

Lower East Side

New York's bargain basement is located in the old Lower East Side immigrant ghetto of tenements, congested workshops and pushcarts. This is the area that spawned some of America's greatest writers, musicians, actors, politicians and business executives.

Most of the area's 19th-century slums have been replaced by huge housing projects, but vestiges of "the old neighborhood" remain between the large east-west thoroughfares of Houston and Delancey streets and such north-south streets as Essex, Ludlow, Orchard, Allen and Eldridge. Shopping in this yeasty area is basic as well as cut-rate. Merchandise in the incredibly cluttered stores and shops is displayed on overflowing racks, stuffed into shelves, piled into bins, stacked on tables—bursting the confines of the premises and taking over the sidewalks. Decor is a foreign word, and privacy is a concept for your own home—if you want to try on something, duck behind a rack or have a friend block the view.

Wily New York shoppers frequent the Lower East Side for such essentials as linens, lingerie, silver and china, jewelry, opticals, appliances, jeans and shoes, and both men's and women's clothing. The area is open every day except Friday at sundown to Saturday at sundown. The Lower East Side is no longer predominantly Jewish—Hispanics and Asians now share the district—but the religious shopkeepers still observe Orthodox ways and keep the Sabbath holy.

Empire State Building Run-up

Each February, marathon runners take the stairs instead of the elevators in this race staged at the city's 60-year-old landmark skyscraper. Members of the Road Runners Club race up the 1,575 steps to the 86th floor of the Empire State Building.

Chinese New Year

Celebrations in February throughout the city's Chinatown and its satellite communities feature lavish, multicourse banquets in restaurants, lion-dancing processions in the streets and fireworks everywhere.

St. Patrick's Day Parade

Fifth Avenue sports a green stripe for the lively and colorful March St. Patrick's Day Parade—the world's largest and longest—which kicks off at noon and marches for hours, traveling from 44th to 86th streets.

St. Patrick's Day Parade

Easter Parade

On Easter Sunday from late morning to late afternoon, New Yorkers and their guests promenade up and down Fifth Avenue, showing off their new spring outfits and enjoying the fine spring weather. The center is St. Patrick's Cathedral, Fifth Avenue and 50th Street. This is no formal, organized parade, but simply an informal event open to all

Ninth Avenue International Food Festival

Occurring in May, the Ninth Avenue International Food Festival is the city's largest open-air feast. One ethnic food stall after the other stretches from 37th Street to 50th Street all along Ninth Avenue.

Washington Square Outdoor Art Show

For three weekends in late May and early June, this huge art show originates at 4th Street and Fifth Avenue and takes over the sidewalks of all streets in and around Washington Square in Greenwich Village.

The Festival of St. Anthony of Padua

Every June, this wonderful street festival of Italian food and fun turns the normally quiet neighborhood of the South Village into a night-and-day carnival. It starts at the Church of St. Anthony at Sullivan and Houston streets.

Ninth Avenue International Food Festival

Metropolitan Opera Concerts in the Parks

Metropolitan Opera Concerts in the Parks

The free summertime Metropolitan Opera concerts in the parks of all five boroughs are concert versions of Met productions with top stars of the company—internationally famous names such as Luciano Pavarotti, Kathleen Battle, Jessye Norman, Placido Domingo and Frederica von Stade—who perform with a full Metropolitan orchestra under the baton of such leading conductors as James Levine, James Conlon and Charles MacKerras. The stars appear in formal attire and perform on a high-tech, state-of-the-art mobile stage that guarantees the best possible sound in the open air. Spectators sit on the grass—in Central Park on the Great Lawn—or on blankets, and many bring elaborate picnic suppers to add to the festive nature of the evening.

Shakespeare Performers in the Park

Two of Shakespeare's plays are staged every summer in the open-air Delacorte Theater in Central Park (enter 81st Street from either the east or west side of the park). Joseph Papp, director of the New York Shakespeare Festival, began the series in the 1950s, and his productions are so popular that people start lining up hours ahead of time for the free tickets, which are passed out at 6 p.m. Top stars appear in the plays—recent examples are Michelle Pfeiffer, Morgan Freeman, Kevin Kline, Linda Rondstadt and Tracey Ullman—and the sets, costumes and lighting are all of the highest quality.

July Fourth Festival

In New York July Fourth is celebrated with enthusiasm and excitement. The entire Lower Manhattan historic area is the focal point of the festivities. These include a Harbor Festival of yacht and boat races on the bay and rivers, a Great July Fourth Festival on land, the annual Macy's Fireworks spectacular on the East River and all manner of activities—including concerts and more fireworks—at the South Street Seaport. In Staten Island, historic, restored Richmondtown is the scene of the annual Independence Day Ice Cream Social.

Lincoln Center Out-of-Doors Festival

Every performance of the Lincoln Center Out-of-Doors Festival—which is staged every day throughout the month of August—is free. Jazz, clown theater, children's theater, classical and folk music, classical and modern dance, mime shows and plays—all are presented in the parks and plaza of the huge Lincoln Center complex. Major productions are given in the large outdoor Damrosch Band Shell; smaller events are given around the central fountain in the plaza area. Groups include such renowned performers as the Joffrey Ballet, the Alvin Ailey Dance Theater and musicians from the popular "Mostly Mozart" series.

Harlem Week

Actually a two-week festival in August culminating in Harlem Day, Harlem Week was founded in the mid-1970s to focus attention on the cultural, social and economic life of the Capital of Black America. Reggae, calypso, blues, gospel and Latin music are performed in various locations throughout the Harlem area. Fashion shows are staged by the Harlem Institute of Fashion, and an annual Black Film Festival recognizes the contributions of black actors and filmmakers. The festival has events for children, teen-agers, seniors and families. There are food fairs and sports events—especially the Golden Hoops basketball competition and the NBA Pro/Am playoffs. Harlem Day—always on a Sunday—is a daylong celebration with numerous events taking place along 125th and 135th streets.

Feast of San Gennaro

This blockbuster Italian street fair is held in Lower Manhattan for 10 mid-September days from noon to midnight. A wonderful, colorful Italian celebration, this festival features sumptuous Italian food and mementos.

The Big Apple Circus

This delightful, small-scale, one-ring circus from the New York School for Circus Arts has become a tradition in New York. It sets up its intimate tent every year in Lincoln Center's Damrosch Park, late fall to January.

Greenwich Village Halloween Parade

More than a march—it's an October community event, a celebration of the imagination and freedom of expression for which the Village is noted. *Everyone* is invited to join the procession, and the costumes—always topical, satirical and, in many cases, political—range from beautiful to bizarre.

New York City Marathon

November's first weekend brings the mammoth, 25,000-runner event, which travels through all five boroughs of the city, over five bridges, in its 26.2-mile race to the finish line in Central Park.

Macy's Thanksgiving Day Parade

The lavish parade is the city's most elaborate, most beloved procession, especially for families with small children. The giant balloons of a host of cartoon figures must be seen to be believed. The route is Central Park West and 77th Street down Broadway to Herald Square. Santa Claus is always the last float, signaling the beginning of the year-end holiday season.

Manhattan Antiques and Collectibles Show

A huge exposition attracting antiques and collectibles buyers and sellers from all over the world, this show occupies three Hudson River piers for the last two weekends of November.

Holiday Celebrations

The gala holiday season in New York kicks off with the lighting of the giant Christmas tree in Rockefeller Center and the lighting of the Giant Hanukkah Menorah at Grand Army Plaza, Fifth Avenue and 59th Street. The New York City Ballet performs "The Nutcracker," the Hayden Planetarium presents "Christmas Star Show" sky show, and dozens of other celebrations salute the holiday season.

On New Year's Eve, at 42nd Street and Broadway, look up to the top of No. 1 Times Square. Every December 31st an illuminated ball drops from the roof at midnight while millions of revelers jam the area to cheer in the new year with horns, whistles and loud cheers. The custom started when The New York Times moved into the 25-story tower on December 31, 1904, and marked the occasion with fanfare and fireworks. Since then Times Square and New Year's Eve have been synonymous.

Greenwich Village

The charming and eccentric neighborhood that is the birthplace of New York City's cultural life began as an Indian village, was converted to farmland in the 17th century, became an area of country homes during the 18th century, was established as the city's most fashionable neighborhood in the 19th century, and developed into a creative cauldron of artists, writers and musicians during the early 20th century. Always a residential district—the city's commercial interests skipped over it as they moved steadily north—the Village looks much today as it did when its well-preserved Federal and Italianate townhouses were built during the early to late 19th century.

Walking is the only way to explore the Village's crazy-quilt streets—the grid system also skipped over the Village when the city was laid out. The usual starting point is Washington Square at the foot of Fifth Avenue. Now a lovely park of venerable trees, dignified statues, a central fountain and monumental Washington Arch, the square was once a potter's field, a parade ground and an execution spot (the ancient elm in the northwest corner was called "the hanging tree"). Along the square's north side is "The Row," a series of handsome Greek Revival townhouses, once the homes of such notables as Edith Wharton, Edmund Wilson and Henry James' grandmother (whose home inspired the author's novel "Washington Square"). Today the houses—and most of the buildings around the square—are owned by New York University.

The most delightful Village streets to explore lie west of Washington Square—in fact, west of Seventh Avenue. On your way over to them, you'll pass by several landmarks. The Jefferson Market Courthouse Library at Sixth Avenue and 10th Street is a strange-looking "Venetian Gothic" brick building with a tall tower that once served as a fire lookout. The 1827 Northern Dispensary, a triangular brick building of Georgian design, is where poet Edgar Allan Poe went for his aspirin tablets. Sheridan Square, another village rallying point, contains two parks: triangular Christopher Park, with its statue of Civil War Gen. Philip Sheridan, and Sheridan Square, a triangular, fenced-in garden just around the corner.

You could spend days strolling through the streets west of Sheridan Square; but if time is limited, don't miss these two gems. Grove Court is a lovely cul-de-sac off the side street between Bedford and Hudson streets whose tiny brick houses were the setting of the O. Henry short story "The New Leaf." St. Luke's Place between Seventh Avenue South and Hudson Street is where poet Marianne Moore and former Mayor Jimmy Walker once lived. One of these houses is the Huxtable family's home on "The Cosby Show."

Grove Court

Statue of George M. Cohan

Old St. Peter's Church

Times Square

Stroll up Broadway from Times Square and 42nd Street to about 53rd Street. Poke into the side streets, east and west, where most of the area's theaters are located (only a few, such as the Marquis, the Winter Garden and the Broadway, are actually on Broadway). Notice all the new buildings—new hotels, shops and restaurants—that are making up what's called The Times Square Renaissance.

Historic spots to look for as you walk through the Broadway theater district include the triangular Duffy Square, Broadway between 46th and 47th streets. At the northern end is the TKTS booth for half-price tickets and behind it is a statue of World War I hero Father Francis P. Duffy, the Fighting Chaplain of New York's famed 69th Regiment, who was later a friend of writers and actors as pastor of Holy Cross Church on West 42nd Street. At the southern end is a statue of playwright/actor George M. Cohan, who wrote the immortal "Give My Regards to Broadway." At the southeast corner of Broadway and 44th Street is a plaque marking the birthplace of America's greatest playwright, Eugene O'Neill, who was born in a hotel that once stood here; and across the street is 1501 Broadway, the building that once held the famous Paramount Theater, where the young Frank Sinatra once sang to packed houses of hysterical bobby-soxers. You can just make out the now-reconstructed, two-story entrance of the old movie palace.

Lower Manhattan and Financial District

The Big Apple was planted in Lower Manhattan. The Dutch were the first to establish a colony (New Amsterdam) in the first part of the 17th century; then the English took over in 1664, renaming the colony for the Duke of York. Independence came in 1776, and George Washington took the oath of office at Federal Hall on April 30, 1789.

Essential historic sites in Lower Manhattan include the still-operating 1719 Fraunces Tavern at Broad and Pearl streets, where George Washington bade farewell to his troops in 1783. The 1837 Old St. Peter's Church at Barclay and Church streets is New York State's oldest Roman Catholic parish; it was attended by Mother Seaton (1774–1821) and Pierre Toussaint (1766–1853).

The best overview of this historic area is from the observation deck on the 107th floor of No. 2 World Trade Center. Back down at ground level, walk through the lobby of No. 1 World Trade Center and over the enclosed North Bridge to the World Financial Center/Battery Park City (completed in the late 1980s) for a look at the *new* New York—a $4 billion, 21st-century "city built onto a city."

SoHo 20 Gallery

SoHo

The principal attractions of SoHo are its cast-iron architecture, its numerous art galleries, its shops—mainly for trendy clothing—and its restaurants, largely Italian and French.

SoHo also has a fascinating history, traces of which you should look for as you explore the district's streets. In the 17th century many of the area's residents were blacks set free by the controlling Dutch West India Company in 1644, and in the 18th century the neighborhood was one of the city's most fashionable residential areas. In the 19th century commerce arrived in the form of stores, theaters, restaurants, hotels and vices (a "Madame Sweet" was in business at 25 Wooster St., described as "a very dashing paw-paw establishment" in an 1839 court case).

Feel free to walk into any of the many art galleries and browse the pictures, photographs and sculptures for as long as you wish; no one will press you to buy, although price lists are readily available upon request. Usually you can tell by looking through the large street windows what artworks merit closer inspection, but several galleries shouldn't be missed. Leo Castelli, who pioneered in such modern giants as Andy Warhol, Jasper Johns and Robert Rauschenberg, has his downtown gallery at 420 W. Broadway, the area's main north-south avenue. His former partner, Ivan Karp, now runs his own gallery, the O.K. Harris, at 383 W. Broadway; his exhibitions are always fascinating—often startling. The New Renaissance Gallery at 382 W. Broadway receives hundreds of artists' portfolios each year, from international as well as American artists, and selects a dozen or so for special exhibit.

New Renaissance Gallery

O.K. Harris Gallery

TriBeCa

Shaped roughly like a triangle below Canal Street (hence the name), TriBeCa began as a satellite to its neighbor SoHo. Quieter and much less commercial than SoHo, TriBeCa nevertheless contains some of New York's finest restaurants and a number of art galleries, the spillover from the proliferation in SoHo.

Its buildings are TriBeCa's real treasure. Unlike SoHo, which is predominantly cast-iron, TriBeCa boasts a marvelous mixture of 19th-century architecture, from modest Federal townhouses on far west Harrison Street to the massive American Thread Building at 260 W. Broadway, which is now converted to deluxe condos.

One of Manhattan's oldest districts, TriBeCa was once an area of 17th-century Dutch farms, the last remnant of which is tiny, triangular Duane Park—look for the plaque that tells its history. Until the middle of the present century, this district was the Washington Market wholesale food center. All traces of this activity have vanished except for a few old signs and faded lettering on the sides of buildings, but the name is commemorated in beautifully landscaped Washington Market Park. This park is a part of the huge, three-tower apartment complex called Independence Plaza.

Other significant TriBeCa landmarks include the 19th-century studio of Civil War photographer Mathew Brady at 359 Broadway and the Hotel Bond, 125 Chambers St., which is probably the city's oldest and supposedly the first to offer room telephones and room service.

American Thread Building

General Theological Seminary

Chelsea

Like Greenwich Village, its southern neighbor, the west-side district of Chelsea has always been a largely residential neighborhood. Much of the area (between 14th and 34th streets, Fifth Avenue and the Hudson River) was once owned by the family of Clement Clarke Moore, author of "A Visit from St. Nicholas," or "'Twas the Night Before Christmas," as we know it today. When the Moore estate was broken up, the neatly patterned grid streets and 19th-century townhouses we see today established the section's character.

Streets to explore in the Chelsea Historic District are 20th, 21st and 22nd streets between Eighth and Tenth avenues. Here you'll find a concentration of townhouses, churches and other landmarks. Chelsea's oldest house is marked with a plaque at the northwest corner of 21st Street and Ninth Avenue. The 1836–1900 General Theological Seminary, between Ninth and Tenth avenues and 20th and 21st streets, looks like a building out of a Charles Dickens novel. St. Peter's Church, 344 W. 20th St., is an 1836–1838 church built from designs by Clement Clarke Moore and graced by original Tiffany stained-glass windows.

Chelsea is rich in theatrical and literary history. Sarah Bernhardt performed there; British actress Lily Langtry lived there; and Adele and Fred Astaire practiced dance steps in an old studio. Writers associated with Chelsea, at one time or another, include Stephen Crane, Sherwood Anderson, Wallace Stevens, Jack Kerouac, William Saroyan, Mark Twain, Thomas Wolfe, Dylan Thomas, Brendan Behan, Arthur Miller and Tennessee Williams. Many of them stayed in the magnificent 1884 Victorian Gothic Chelsea Hotel, still open for business at 23rd Street, just off Seventh Avenue.

Chelsea Historic District

Chinatown

Manhattan's Chinatown is a compact, well-defined area. Canal Street is the northern boundary, Worth Street marks the southern boundary, with Mulberry Street and the Bowery roughly setting the west and east boundaries. Expansion, however, is breaking the borders, especially to the north and east; and Chinese signs have been appearing in increasing numbers throughout Little Italy, Chinatown's next-door neighbor.

As you stroll around the narrow, crowded streets, soaking up the exotic atmosphere, you can shop for unusual gifts and souvenirs that are usually inexpensive. Shopping suggestions include china and porcelain objects, lanterns, fans, joss sticks (incense), fanciful kites, Chinese blouses and robes and, naturally, chopsticks.

During your self-guided walking tour, notice the unusual fruits and vegetables in the fresh produce markets—Chinese cabbage, bean sprouts, winter melons and colorful squashes. Marvel at the roasted Peking ducks you'll see hanging upside down in the meat markets. A few historic sights include Olliffe's Pharmacy at 6 Bowery, the oldest (1803) drugstore in America; 15 Bowery, the site of a cheap rooming house where composer Stephen Collins Foster lived in 1864; and 6 Doyers St., which once held a club that hired Irving Berlin as a singing waiter.

Chinese New Year celebration

95

Old police headquarters at 240 Centre St.

Little Italy

Most of the Italian residents of Little Italy trace their roots to Naples, Calabria and Sicily, so the restaurants they established in New York are decidedly southern in flavor: gutsy and garlic-infused. The waiters are friendly—even flirty with the ladies—and all the diners are invited to have an uninhibited good time.

Normally, Little Italy's streets are quieter than Chinatown, but they explode with carnival excitement during the annual street feast of San Gennaro, the patron saint of Naples, during early September. Food stalls line both sides of all the streets, and pedestrians pass down the midway between the coiled sausages, clams and calamari, all types of pasta, pastries and pizza.

The most historic structure in Little Italy is Old St. Patrick's Cathedral (1809) at the corner of Prince and Mott streets. The resorted structure, a Georgian-Gothic gem, continues to serve its community long after the cardinal's seat moved to Fifth Avenue and 50th Street in 1879. Another architectural treasure is the former police headquarters at 240 Centre St.; this elaborate Beaux Arts–style structure, with its columned clock dome, was built between 1905 and 1909 to resemble London's Old Bailey. Now converted into posh cooperative apartments, the historic building once held such unsavory characters as Legs Diamond, Gyp the Blood and Two-Gun Crowley.